GIFTS & CALLING

DISCOVERING GOD'S WILL

	ENTRY LEVEL	ADVANCED LEVEL
SESSION 1 Getting Acquainted	Called by God Luke 5:1–11	
SESSION 2 Hearing God's Call	Called in a New Direction Acts 16:6–10	Called to a New Life 1 Cor. 1:18–2:5
SESSION 3 Discovering Our Gifts	Signs for Moses Exodus 4:1–17	Living Sacrifices Romans 12:1–8
SESSION 4 Developing Our Gifts	A Division of Duties Acts 6:1–7	A Variety of Gifts 1 Corinthians 12:7–27
SESSION 5 Taking Risks	The Risk of Investment Matthew 25:14–30	No More Timidity 2 Timothy 1:3–14
SESSION 6 Reflecting On Work	Workers in the Vineyard Matthew 20:1–16	Future Plans James 4:13–17
SESSION 7 Having a Servant Mind	The Example of Christ John 13:1–17	The Attitude of Christ Philippians 2:1–11

Serendipity House / P.O. Box 1012 / Littleton, CO 80160

TOLL FREE 1-800-525-9563 / www.serendipityhouse.com

99 00 01 / **101 series • CHG** / 4 3

PROJECT ENGINEER:
Lyman Coleman

WRITING TEAM:
Richard Peace, Lyman Coleman, Matthew Lockhart, Andrew Sloan, Cathy Tardif

PRODUCTION TEAM:
Christopher Werner, Sharon Penington, Erika Tiepel

COVER PHOTO:
© 1998 D. Boone / Westlight

CORE VALUES

Community: The purpose of this curriculum is to build community within the body of believers around Jesus Christ.

Group Process: To build community, the curriculum must be designed to take a group through a step-by-step process of sharing your story with one another.

Interactive Bible Study: To share your "story," the approach to Scripture in the curriculum needs to be open-ended and right brain—to "level the playing field" and encourage everyone to share.

Developmental Stages: To provide a healthy program in the life cycle of a group, the curriculum needs to offer courses on three levels of commitment: (1) Beginner Stage—low-level entry, high structure, to level the playing field; (2) Growth Stage— deeper Bible study, flexible structure, to encourage group accountability; (3) Discipleship Stage—in-depth Bible study, open structure, to move the group into high gear.

Target Audiences: To build community throughout the culture of the church, the curriculum needs to be flexible, adaptable and transferable into the structure of the average church.

ACKNOWLEDGMENTS

To Zondervan Bible Publishers
for permission to use
the NIV text,
The Holy Bible, New International Bible Society.
© 1973, 1978, 1984 by International Bible Society.
Used by permission of Zondervan Bible Publishers.

Questions and Answers

PURPOSE

1. What is the purpose of this group?

In a nutshell, the purpose is to get acquainted and to double the size of the group.

STAGE

2. What stage in the life cycle of a small group is this course designed for?

This 101 course is designed for the first stage in the three-stage life cycle of a small group. (See diagram below.) For a full explanation of the three-stage life cycle, see the center section.

GOALS

3. What is the purpose of stage one in the life cycle?

The focus in this first stage is primarily on Group Building.

GROUP BUILDING

4. How does this course develop Group Building?

Take a look at the illustration of the baseball diamond on page M5 in the center section. In the process of using this course, you will go around the four bases.

BIBLE STUDY

5. What is the approach to Bible Study in this course?

As shown on page M4 of the center section, there are two tracks in this book. Track 1 is the light option, based on stories in the Bible. Track 2 is the heavier option, based on teaching passages in the Bible.

THREE-STAGE LIFE CYCLE OF A GROUP

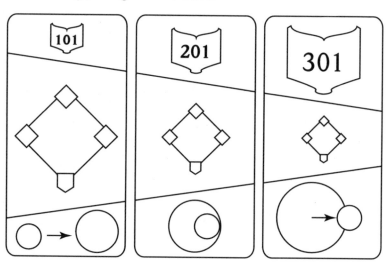

**CHOOSING
A TRACK**

6. Which option of Bible Study is best for our group?

Track 1 is the best option for people not familiar with the Bible, as well as for groups who are not familiar with each other. Track 2 is the best option for groups who are familiar with the Bible *and* with one another. (However, whenever you have new people come to a meeting, we recommend you switch to Track 1 for that Bible Study.)

**CHOOSING
BOTH OPTIONS**

7. Can we choose both options?

Yes, depending upon your time schedule. Here's how to decide:

STUDY	APPROXIMATE COMPLETION TIME
Story Sharing only	60–90 minutes
Epistle Study only	60–90 minutes
Story and Epistle Study	90–120 minutes

**13-WEEK
PLAN**

8. What if we want to do both the Story and Epistle Studies but don't have time at the session?

You can spend two weeks on a unit—the Story Questionnaire the first week and the Epistle Study the next. Session 1 has only one Bible Study—so you would end up with 13 weeks if you followed this plan.

**BIBLE
KNOWLEDGE**

9. What if you don't know anything about the Bible?

No problem. The Story option is based on a parable or story that stands on its own—to discuss as though you are hearing it for the first time. The Epistle Study comes complete with reference notes—to help you understand the context of the Bible passage and any difficult words that need to be defined.

THE FEARLESS FOURSOME!

If you have more than seven people at a meeting, Serendipity recommends you divide into groups of 4 for the Bible Study. Count off around the group: "one, two, one, two, etc."—and have the "ones" move quickly to another room for the Bible Study. Ask one person to be the leader and follow the directions for the Bible Study time. After 30 minutes, the Group Leader will call "Time" and ask all groups to come together for the Caring Time.

10. **What is the mission of a 101 group?**

Turn to page M5 of the center section. This course is designed for groups in the Birth stage—which means that your mission is to increase the size of the group by filling the "empty chair."

11. **How do we fill the empty chair?**

Pull up an empty chair during the group's prayer time and ask God to bring a new person to the group to fill it.

12. **What is a group covenant?**

A group covenant is a "contract" that spells out your expectations and the ground rules for your group. It's very important that your group discuss these issues—preferably as part of the first session.

13. **What are the ground rules for the group?** (Check those that you agree upon.)

❏ PRIORITY: While you are in the course, you give the group meetings priority.

❏ PARTICIPATION: Everyone participates and no one dominates.

❏ RESPECT: Everyone is given the right to their own opinion and all questions are encouraged and respected.

❏ CONFIDENTIALITY: Anything that is said in the meeting is never repeated outside the meeting.

❏ EMPTY CHAIR: The group stays open to new people at every meeting.

❏ SUPPORT: Permission is given to call upon each other in time of need—even in the middle of the night.

❏ ADVICE GIVING: Unsolicited advice is not allowed.

❏ MISSION: We agree to do everything in our power to start a new group as our mission (see center section).

Getting Acquainted

3-PART AGENDA

ICE-BREAKER
15 Minutes

BIBLE STUDY
30 Minutes

CARING TIME
15–45 Minutes

Welcome to a group where together we will explore the topic of our "gifts and calling." Our gifts and calling are central elements of our uniqueness as people. Our gifts are the specific, Spirit-given abilities which enable us to contribute to the wider good of the community and world. Our calling is the task or area of service where God directs us to use those gifts. Our calling is sometimes called our "vocation." At times, that word is too closely identified with a paid job. Our calling may or may not be the same thing as our paid job. Sometimes a calling is something we need to do as a volunteer.

According to a survey done by James Patterson and Peter Kim for their book *The Day America Told the Truth,* many people do not see their present work as a true vocation. Consider these statistics from that survey:

- Only 1 in 4 people work to achieve their potential rather than to merely keep food on the table.
- Only 1 in 4 people give work their best effort.
- Only 1 in 10 say they are satisfied with their jobs.
- Almost half of American workers admit to chronic malingering (calling in sick when they are not sick, and doing it regularly).

LEADER: Be sure to read the "Questions and Answers" on pages 3–5. Take some time during this first session to have the group go over the ground rules on page 5. At the beginning of the Caring Time have your group look at pages M1–M3 in the center section of this book.

It can be difficult for many of us to determine our calling. How do we know what God is calling us to do? Some people have a strong sense of this in high school; others do not discover it until well into adulthood. Former tennis great Arthur Ashe (who died in 1993) was looking for his vocation *after* his tennis career was over, and even after he contracted AIDS from a blood transfusion. He wrote in his book *Days of Grace:* "If God hadn't put me on this earth mainly to stroke tennis balls, he certainly hadn't put me here to be greedy. I wanted to make a difference, however small, in the world, and I wanted to do so in a useful and honorable way."

The focus of this course is to help us search together for how we can:
- Hear God's call
- Discover our gifts
- Develop our gifts
- Take risks
- Reflect on our work
- Have a servant mind

In this course we want to learn about the Bible, but we want to do so in a way that sheds light on who we are. The focus, then, will be on telling your story and using the passage as a springboard.

Every session has three parts: (1) **Ice-Breaker**—to break the ice and introduce the topic, (2) **Bible Study**—to share your life through a passage of Scripture, and (3) **Caring Time**—to share prayer concerns and pray for one another.

Ice-Breaker / 15 Minutes

The Old Neighborhood. Take some time to share with each other your "old neighborhood." If you moved a lot, talk about the neighborhood where you spent the most time, or the one which was your favorite. On the other hand, you may still be living in your old neighborhood.

1. Where was your "old neighborhood"?

2. Which of the following was your old neighborhood like?
   ❏ Sesame Street—urban and multicultural
   ❏ Fat Albert's neighborhood—distinctively ethnic
   ❏ Home Improvement—suburban housing with a common cultural background
   ❏ The Waltons—rural and spread out, but close-knit

3. Respond to as many of the following as you have time for:
   ❏ Where did the kids gather in your neighborhood?
   ❏ What were your favorite things to do together?
   ❏ Where were the special places—the best climbing trees, the best swimming holes? The places you could go to hide from adults?
   ❏ Where were the "danger spots"—the yards with mean dogs, the "grumpy old Mr. Wilson" who didn't like kids, the "haunted" houses?
   ❏ Who was the "Dennis the Menace" who always got into trouble or got you into trouble?
   ❏ Who were the kids who really stood out from the rest of the crowd—the "Weird Harolds" and "Fat Alberts"?

Bible Study / 30 Minutes

Luke 5:1–11 / Called by God

In this first session, you will have a chance to share about God's call in your life. This passage is from the beginning of Jesus' ministry and focuses on the calling of his first disciples. Ask one person to read Luke 5:1–11 out loud. Then discuss the questions with your group. Be sure to save time at the close to discuss the issues in the Caring Time.

5 *One day as Jesus was standing by the Lake of Gennesaret, with the people crowding around him and listening to the word of God, ²he saw at the water's edge two boats, left there by the fishermen, who were washing their nets. ³He got into one of the boats, the one belonging to Simon, and asked him to put out a little from shore. Then he sat down and taught the people from the boat.*

⁴When he had finished speaking, he said to Simon, "Put out into deep water, and let down the nets for a catch."

⁵Simon answered, "Master, we've worked hard all night and haven't caught anything. But because you say so, I will let down the nets."

⁶When they had done so, they caught such a large number of fish that their nets began to break. ⁷So they signaled their partners in the other boat to come and help them, and they came and filled both boats so full that they began to sink.

⁸When Simon Peter saw this, he fell at Jesus' knees and said, "Go away from me, Lord; I am a sinful man!" ⁹For he and all his companions were astonished at the catch of fish they had taken, ¹⁰and so were James and John, the sons of Zebedee, Simon's partners.

Then Jesus said to Simon, "Don't be afraid; from now on you will catch men." ¹¹So they pulled their boats up on shore, left everything and followed him.

1. If you had been Simon Peter when Jesus said, "Put out into deep water, and let down the nets for a catch," what would you have done?

❑ wondered who this guy thought he was
❑ told Jesus I was too tired since I had worked hard all night
❑ suggested another time when the fish were biting
❑ politely told Jesus to stick to his preaching
❑ grudgingly gone ahead with the idea
❑ happily done what Jesus asked

2. When they caught so many fish that their nets began to break, how do you think Peter felt?

❏ overjoyed   ❏ terrible about what he had said

❏ dumbfounded   ❏ aware of who Jesus was

3. How do these fishermen's decisions to leave everything strike you?

❏ How silly to give up a respectable career for who knows what!

❏ How exciting to try something new!

❏ It would take a lot more than this to get me to change careers.

❏ Following Jesus is more important than any career.

4. When was the first time you felt the tug of Jesus on your heart?

❏ when I was very young   ❏ just recently

❏ in a church service   ❏ I don't know that I have.

❏ when there was a crisis in my life   ❏ other:_____

❏ when I was at a retreat or camp

5. Where are you now in relation to Jesus?

❏ on the shore—a spectator

❏ in the boat—learning who Jesus is

❏ at the helm—letting God take control

❏ on the dock—waiting for something to happen

6. Of the decisions Peter and his friends made, which do you have the hardest time making?

❏ who to serve or follow

❏ where to live and work

❏ what my mission and role is in life

❏ when to begin something new

7. What would it mean for you to be "catching people" for Jesus?

❏ to share my faith with my friends

❏ to invite friends to my church

❏ to show others God's love through *my* love

❏ to start focusing on people rather than things

8. In order to "catch people" for Jesus, what do you have going for you that is good "bait" (something that helps draw people to Jesus)?

❏ my ability to make friends

❏ my ability to share my faith

❏ my ability to listen to people's problems

❏ my knowledge of the Bible

❏ my willingness to "walk my talk"

❏ my willingness to help people in need

❏ other:_____

"It never cost a disciple anything to follow Jesus: to talk about cost when you are in love with someone is an insult."
—Oswald Chambers

9

9. How would you characterize your follow-through on your call to be a disciple?

❐ Jesus is my Lord, and I follow him daily.

❐ Jesus is a great rabbi (teacher): I listen, but follow when I like.

❐ Jesus is my Savior, but we don't have a close relationship.

❐ Jesus is the Son of God, but not too involved in my daily life.

❐ Jesus is my Messiah, and I'm here to find out what that means.

❐ other:_____

Caring Time / *15–45 Minutes*

LEADER:
Ask the group, "Who are you going to invite next week?"

The most important time in every meeting is this—the Caring Time—where you take time to share prayer requests and pray for one another. To make sure this time is not neglected, you need to set a minimum time that you will devote to prayer requests and prayer and count backward from the closing time by this amount. For instance, if you are going to close at 9 p.m., and you are going to devote 30 minutes to prayer requests and prayer, you need to ask a timekeeper to call "time" at 8:30 and move to prayer requests. Start out by asking everyone to answer this question:

"How can we help you in prayer this week?"

Then, move into prayer. If you have not prayed out loud before, finish these sentences:

"Hello, God, this is ... (first name). I want to thank you for ..."

Be sure to pray for the empty chair. And as you do, think about who you could invite to join you as you begin this study.

GROUP DIRECTORY

P.S.
At the close, pass around your books and have everyone sign the Group Directory inside the front cover.

Hearing God's Call

3-PART AGENDA

ICE-BREAKER
15 Minutes

BIBLE STUDY
30 Minutes

CARING TIME
15–45 Minutes

The things we want to hear are often easy to hear. But there are other times when we long to hear something clearly, and it is much more difficult. Such is the case with hearing God's call. We long for God's direction in life, but find it hard to hear what God is saying to us. This is complicated by the fact that some people (who claim to be following God's direction) do crazy and even violent things. People like David Koresh and Jim Jones make us wary of what it means to hear the voice of God calling us.

However, our lives cannot be guided by pathological aberrations. Too many people have served God and humanity because they heard God's call—people like Billy Graham, Martin Luther King, Jr. and Mother Teresa. There are also many ordinary, less publicized people. These include hospital volunteers, school aides, children's coaches and others who have consistently made a difference in this world.

The question then becomes: How do we hear God's call? How can we differentiate between the voice of God, our own will and all of the other voices which call us in this world? Do we listen for an audible voice? Or do we need to pay attention to the more subtle things around us and within us?

LEADER: *If there are new people in this session, review the ground rules for this group on page 5. Have the group look at page M4 in the center section and decide which Bible Study option to use— light or heavy. If you have more than seven people, see the box about the "Fearless Foursome" on page 4.*

In this session, we will look at this issue of hearing God's call. In the Option 1 Study, we will look at a story from Acts—how the apostle Paul was planning to go one way, but was called by God in another direction. We will talk about how he discerned that call, and what it means for us to discern God's call. In the Option 2 Study (from Paul's first letter to the Corinthians), we will consider the difference between what the world calls us to and what God calls us to.

Ice-Breaker / 15 Minutes

Like Music to My Ears. In each of the following pairs, which sound is more likely to be "music to your ears"? Go down this list one at a time and share your choice with the group.

the crackling of a campfire	the sounds of city traffic at night
the cry of "play ball!"	waves crashing against the shore
a train whistle in the distance	the bell of an ice cream truck
the ring of the telephone	the ring of a cash register
the gurgling of a mountain stream	the buzz of an opening-night crowd
the purr of a kitten	the hum of a well-tuned engine
the silence of new-fallen snow	the cheering of a crowd
the sound of a gentle rain	the rapid talk of an auctioneer

Bible Study / 30 Minutes

Option 1 / Story Passage

Acts 16:6–10 / Called in a New Direction

This story occurred when the apostle Paul was on a missionary journey to establish new churches. Prior to this, all of the churches he had established had been in the area known as Asia Minor. This call led to the first churches in Europe. Read Acts 16:6–10, and discuss the questions which follow with your group.

⁶Paul and his companions traveled throughout the region of Phrygia and Galatia, having been kept by the Holy Spirit from preaching the word in the province of Asia. ⁷When they came to the border of Mysia, they tried to enter Bithynia, but the Spirit of Jesus would not allow them to. ⁸So they passed by Mysia and went down to Troas. ⁹During the night Paul had a vision of a man of Macedonia standing and begging him, "Come over to Macedonia and help us." ¹⁰After Paul had seen the vision, we got ready at once to leave for Macedonia, concluding that God had called us to preach the gospel to them.

1. From this passage, describe how Paul makes his decisions:
❏ based on impulse and emotion
❏ in a mystical, almost superstitious manner
❏ in a manner that is sensitive to the needs of the moment
❏ in a way that is constantly open to God's guidance

2. Mark an *"X"* on the lines below to indicate how you make decisions:

based on impulse _____ after much consideration

after consulting others _____ based on my own perceptions

based on present circumstances _____ based on future needs

according to logical analysis _____ according to my gut feeling

3. How sure do you think Paul was that this was the right way to go?
❏ not at all sure—He was just guessing.
❏ rather unsure, but willing to take a chance
❏ confident, but realizing he could be wrong
❏ fully confident, knowing this was the right thing to do

4. When was the last time you made a decision that changed the direction of your life or work?
❏ when I got married
❏ when I changed majors in college
❏ when I changed jobs
❏ when I got divorced
❏ when I made my commitment to Christ
❏ other:_____

5. How confident were you at the time that this decision was right?
❏ not at all sure
❏ rather unsure, but willing to take a chance
❏ confident, but realizing I could be wrong
❏ fully confident, knowing this was the right thing to do

6. When a door of opportunity gets slammed shut in your life, what are you most likely to do?
   ❐ walk away   ❐ bust down the door
   ❐ keep knocking   ❐ climb through a window

7. What's the closest you have come to having a clear message from God, like Paul's vision?

8. What dream for your future do you feel God may be giving you?

9. What will you look for as you seek to determine if this dream is God's call for your life?
   ❐ if I have a vision in the night (like Paul had at Troas)
   ❐ whether there are any barriers put in my way (like at Bithynia)
   ❐ by the needs of people around me (like the Macedonian)
   ❐ consistency with the values and teachings of Scripture
   ❐ God will have to talk to me directly.
   ❐ other:_____

Option 2 / Epistle Study

1 Corinthians 1:18–2:5 / Called to a New Life

The following passage is from the beginning of Paul's first letter to the church at Corinth. In it, he tries to help his readers understand the difference between what human wisdom says is good, and the life to which God calls us. Read 1 Corinthians 1:18–2:5 and answer the questions which follow with your group.

18For the message of the cross is foolishness to those who are perishing, but to us who are being saved it is the power of God. 19For it is written:

"I will destroy the wisdom of the wise;
*   the intelligence of the intelligent I will frustrate."*

20Where is the wise man? Where is the scholar? Where is the philosopher of this age? Has not God made foolish the wisdom of the world? 21For since in the wisdom of God the world through its wisdom did not know him, God was pleased through the foolishness of what was preached to save those who believe. 22Jews demand miraculous signs and Greeks look for wisdom, 23but we preach Christ crucified: a stumbling block to Jews and foolishness to Gentiles, 24but to those whom God has called, both Jews and Greeks, Christ the power of God and the wisdom of God. 25For the foolish-

ness of God is wiser than man's wisdom, and the weakness of God is stronger than man's strength.

²⁶Brothers, think of what you were when you were called. Not many of you were wise by human standards; not many were influential; not many were of noble birth. ²⁷But God chose the foolish things of the world to shame the wise; God chose the weak things of the world to shame the strong. ²⁸He chose the lowly things of this world and the despised things—and the things that are not—to nullify the things that are, ²⁹so that no one may boast before him. ³⁰It is because of him that you are in Christ Jesus, who has become for us wisdom from God—that is, our righteousness, holiness and redemption. ³¹Therefore, as it is written: "Let him who boasts boast in the Lord."

2 When I came to you, brothers, I did not come with eloquence or superior wisdom as I proclaimed to you the testimony about God. ²For I resolved to know nothing while I was with you except Jesus Christ and him crucified. ³I came to you in weakness and fear, and with much trembling. ⁴My message and my preaching were not with wise and persuasive words, but with a demonstration of the Spirit's power, ⁵so that your faith might not rest on men's wisdom, but on God's power.

1. When you were growing up, who did you think was one of the wisest people on earth?

2. What's one of the best decisions you've made? What's one of the worst?

3. What do you think Paul means when he describes the world's wisdom as "foolish" (1:20–21)?

4. Looking back on the big decisions in your life, did you listen more to the world's wisdom or to the wisdom of God?

5. Why does Paul remind the Corinthian Christians of their previous status (1:26): To shame them? To keep them humble? To remind them of their reliance on Christ for personal worth? To show them what God can do with ordinary people?

6. Why is it that people who are highly intelligent and/or successful so often miss the point of the Cross?

7. What was your life like when you were "called" to Christ? How has your life changed as a result of that new life?

8. What effect should the fact that our calling and our gifts are from God have upon us (1:29–31)? What are you tempted to boast in when you are not boasting "in the Lord"?

9. What is the lesson of this passage for you?

❐ Though others may not see my potential, God knows better.

❐ To hear God's call, I may have to disregard some of what the world says or some of my own "wisdom."

❐ The weakest person with God is stronger than the most powerful person without God.

❐ I may need more humility about worldly accomplishments to truly be used by God.

❐ Regardless of my past or background, God wants to use me in my "sphere of influence."

❐ other:_____

Caring Time / 15–45 Minutes

Take time at the close to share any personal prayer requests. Answer the question:

"How can we help you in prayer this week?"

LEADER: Ask the group, "Who are you going to invite next week?"

Then go around and let each person pray for the person on their right. Finish this sentence:

"Dear God, I want to speak to you about my friend _____."

During your prayer time, remember to pray for the empty chair and for the growth of your group.

Reference Notes

Summary. Paul explains in verses 18–25 the difference between human and divine wisdom. He shows that the Gospel is decidedly not a type of human philosophy, because it involves such a reversal of human expectation. Who would have thought that God would work through the scandal of the Cross? Paul then goes on to "prove" that God does indeed work through weakness. He first looks at the Corinthians (vv. 26–31), and then at himself (2:1–5). He points out that they were not very clever and he was not very persuasive. So the fact that they are Christians "proves" that God works through weakness. How else could the fact of the church of Corinth be explained?

1:18 *the message of the cross.* This is the only legitimate slogan. Paul puts the issue in stark terms: the question of eternal destiny centers on the meaning of the Cross. Their misunderstanding and division is no slight matter. It strikes at the core of the Gospel.

foolishness. It is absurd to many that God's redemptive activity involves death by crucifixion.

1:22 *Jews demand miraculous signs.* The Jews expected a Messiah who would come in obvious power doing miraculous deeds. In Jesus they saw one so weak that his enemies got away with killing him. "To the Jew, a crucified Messiah was an impossible contradiction, like 'cooked ice' " (Fee).

Greeks look for wisdom. Their delight was in clever, cunning logic delivered with soaring persuasiveness. That a Jewish peasant who died as a convicted criminal could be the focus of God's redemptive plan was so silly to them as to be laughable.

1:23 To accept the Cross is to accept that people cannot understand God on their own nor find ways to reach him by themselves. They must trust God, not human wisdom and power.

stumbling block. Literally, a scandal. Jesus' crucifixion "proved" to the Jews that he could not be of God (since Deut. 21:23 says those hanging from a tree are cursed of God). A suffering, dying Messiah was totally outside first-century Jewish expectations.

foolishness. Both the Incarnation and Crucifixion are totally unexpected.

1:24 In fact, Christ is both the sign that is craved by the Jews (he is the power of God) and the ultimate truth desired by the Greeks (he is the wisdom of God).

1:26 *think of what you were.* In their own calling they see the paradox of the all-powerful God using the "weak things of the world."

Not many. The early church had special appeal to the poor and to those with little social standing. This was part of its offensiveness—the "wrong" people were attracted to it.

1:27 *the foolish things of the world.* Those who in the estimation of the current culture were insignificant.

to shame. By proving that the wise men were, in fact, quite wrong.

1:29 A church composed of such folk ought to have a better grasp of what the Gospel is all about. To boast is to wrongly evaluate one's own gifts, to put confidence in them, and to express this with a tinge of pride. Such boasting, however, was one of the problems in the Corinthian church.

1:30 *wisdom from God.* Paul spoke of "human wisdom" in verse 17, i.e., philosophical wisdom. But here he begins to "de-philosophize" *sophia* (wisdom) and instead historicize it. The historical Jesus is God's wisdom. It is Christ who mediates God's plan of salvation.

righteousness. Christ is their righteousness in that he took upon himself the guilt of human sin. So on the Last Day when Christians stand before the Judge they are viewed as being "in Christ."

holiness. Human beings cannot come before a holy God because they are not holy; but once again, Christ provides what people lack. His holiness suffices for them and so a relationship with God is assured.

redemption. It is by Christ's redeeming work on the cross that wisdom, righteousness and holiness are mediated to humankind.

2:1 *eloquence or superior wisdom.* "The two nouns are close together in meaning, for eloquence … here is rational talk, and wisdom worldly cleverness. They represent the outward and inward means by which men may commend a case, effectiveness of language, and skill of argumentation" (Barrett).

2:2 In Corinth, a city teeming with articulate philosophers, Paul's refusal to use persuasive speech and brilliant logic in his evangelism was especially striking. Instead, he simply preached the crucified Christ.

2:3 Not for his safety, but because of the awesome responsibility he had to preach the Gospel.

2:4 *demonstration of the Spirit's power.* Paul reveals the secret behind the impact that his preaching made. People were moved by the convicting power of the Holy Spirit. This is the real proof of the validity of the Gospel.

GROUP DIRECTORY

P.S.
If you have a new person in your group, be sure to add their name to the group directory inside the front cover.

SESSION

3

Discovering Our Gifts

3-PART AGENDA

ICE-BREAKER
15 Minutes

BIBLE STUDY
30 Minutes

CARING TIME
15–45 Minutes

Integrally related to hearing God's call is discovering our gifts. There are differences of opinion among Christians about spiritual gifts—what they are, how they are received, and how they should be used. But there is also virtual agreement that God does give all believers spiritual gifts and that these gifts should be used both for God's glory and our fulfillment.

Chariots of Fire was an inspiring movie about Eric Liddell, a runner in the 1924 Olympics. In explaining his success on the track, Liddell, a devout Christian who later became a missionary, said: "When I run, I feel God's pleasure." Part of the adventure of being a Christian is discovering what we do that results in "feeling God's pleasure." How has God made us, gifted us, and called us to use our gifts and abilities?

LEADER: If there are more than seven people at this meeting, divide into groups of 4 for Bible Study. Count off around the group: "one, two, one, two, etc."—and have the "ones" quickly move to another room. When you come back together for the Caring Time, have the group read about your Mission on page M5 of the center section.

In the Option 1 study (from the book of Exodus in the Old Testament), we will look at the story of Moses "discovering" how God was gifting and calling him—though Moses was less than excited about this discovery at first! In the Option 2 study (from Paul's letter to the Romans) we will build upon the following Ice-Breaker, which is based on this passage in Romans 12. Many Bible interpreters and teachers believe that the seven gifts in this passage refer to the "motivational gifts" which affect not only our life calling but shape our very personalities.

Due to the interplay between the Ice-Breaker and the Option 2 study, if your group is using only the Option 1 studies you may want to consider using Option 2 rather than Option 1 for this session. Or you could do both options and spend a total of eight weeks rather than seven in this course.

Ice-Breaker / 15 Minutes

Discovering Your God-Given Gifts. Here is a simple quiz to help you identify some of your spiritual gifts. It focuses on the seven gifts that are mentioned in Romans 12:6–8. For each question, choose the response which best describes you. Ignore the letters in the front of the responses until you have finished answering all the questions. Then tabulate your scores. Because the Option 2 study builds upon this Ice-Breaker, your group may want to do the Option 2 study.

1. Would you consider it more loving and caring to:
   P ☐ help a person to change for the better (or)
   S ☒ do something to meet a special need he or she has?

2. Are you more likely to find fulfillment in a:
   T ☐ teaching career (or)
   G ☒ business venture?

3. To form an opinion about something, would you probably:
   P ☒ go by what you feel and/or believe already (or)
   T ☐ research it until you are confident enough?

4. Would you rather encourage people to:
   G ☐ give generously to a ministry (or)
   C ☒ minister directly to those who are hurting?

5. Would you rather:
   P ☐ pray for someone (or)
   G ☒ provide for him or her?

6. In counseling people, do you:
   P ☐ tell them where they are wrong and what to do (or)
   E ☒ accept them where they are, then suggest change?

7. Would you rather:
   T ☒ train others to do a job (or)
   A ☐ delegate work to others?

8. Would you rather spend time:
   P ☐ in prayer (or)
   A ☒ organizing a Christian project?

9. Is your decision-making:
   T ☒ based on research (or)
   C ☐ difficult for you?

10. Would you rather:
G ☐ financially assist an ongoing project (or)
A ☒ organize the next project?

11. Would you rather participate in:
P ☐ an intercessory prayer group (or)
C ☒ a program to help the poor?

12. Would you rather help someone in need by:
S ☒ doing something for him or her (or)
G ☐ anonymously giving money?

13. Would you prefer to:
E ☐ do individual counseling (or)
A ☒ manage a group project?

14. Would you rather:
S ☒ help set up for or serve a church dinner (or)
T ☐ speak to the group after dinner?

15. If a room needed to be cleaned, would you:
S ☒ get a broom and sweep it (or)
A ☐ figure out who could do the job best?

16. Do you encourage people:
E ☐ by sharing your own experiences (or)
G ☒ by giving them practical help?

17. Would you prefer to spend your time:
A ☒ organizing people and projects (or)
C ☐ ministering to someone in distress?

18. Are you:
E ☒ likely to see a problem as a challenge (or)
C ☐ sometimes overwhelmed by a problem?

19. Would you rather:
S ☒ help with a church work party (or)
C ☐ visit the shut-ins?

20. At a meeting, do you feel it is more important to:
S ☒ make sure the room is left in order (or)
E ☐ spend time socializing?

21. Would you prefer to:
T ☒ read a good book (or)
E ☐ be with people?

This inventory focuses on seven spiritual gifts from Romans 12:6–8.

_1_ Prophet / Perceiver (P)   _3_ Giver (G)
_4_ Server (S)   _4_ Administrator / Leader (A)
_3_ Teacher (T)   ___ Compassion / Mercy Person (C)
_2_ Encourager / Exhorter (E)

Count the number of "P's" you checked and put that number on the line next to Prophet / Perceiver. Do the same for the other letters / gifts. When you are done, you will have an idea of what your spiritual gifts may be.

This exercise has been adapted from the book, *Discover Your God-Given Gifts*, by Don and Katie Fortune, Chosen Books / Baker Books, 1987. Used by permission. To order the book or the complete questionnaire or other materials relating to the spiritual gifts, contact the Fortunes at (360) 297-8878, FAX: (360) 297-8865, e-mail: hearttoheart@soundcom.net or write them at PO Box 101, Kingston, WA 98346.

Bible Study / 30 Minutes

Option 1 / Story Passage

Exodus 4:1–17 / Signs for Moses

Moses is one of the most colorful characters in the Bible. He was born to a Hebrew family during the time the Israelites were enslaved in Egypt. Because of Pharaoh's order that baby boys born to the Hebrews had to be killed, Moses' mother put him in a basket in the Nile River. Moses was rescued and adopted by Pharaoh's own daughter! One day, after Moses had grown up, he saw an Egyptian slave driver beating an Israelite. Moses reacted by killing the Egyptian. When Pharaoh heard of this, he tried to kill Moses, but Moses fled to Midian and became a shepherd. As we pick up the story here, God has just revealed himself to Moses at the burning bush—telling him to return to Egypt to lead his fellow Israelites out of bondage.

4 *Moses answered, "What if they do not believe me or listen to me and say, 'The Lord did not appear to you'?"*

²Then the Lord said to him, "What is that in your hand?"

"A staff," he replied.

³The Lord said, "Throw it on the ground."

Moses threw it on the ground and it became a snake, and he ran from it. ⁴Then the Lord said to him, "Reach out your hand and take it by the tail." So Moses reached out and took hold of the snake and it turned back into a staff in his hand. ⁵"This," said the Lord, "is so that they may believe that the

LORD, the God of their fathers—the God of Abraham, the God of Isaac and the God of Jacob—has appeared to you."

⁶Then the LORD said, "Put your hand inside your cloak." So Moses put his hand into his cloak, and when he took it out, it was leprous, like snow.

⁷"Now put it back into your cloak," he said. So Moses put his hand back into his cloak, and when he took it out, it was restored, like the rest of his flesh.

⁸Then the LORD said, "If they do not believe you or pay attention to the first miraculous sign, they may believe the second. ⁹But if they do not believe these two signs or listen to you, take some water from the Nile and pour it on the dry ground. The water you take from the river will become blood on the ground."

¹⁰Moses said to the LORD, "O LORD, I have never been eloquent, neither in the past nor since you have spoken to your servant. I am slow of speech and tongue."

¹¹The LORD said to him, "Who gave man his mouth? Who makes him deaf or mute? Who gives him sight or makes him blind? Is it not I, the LORD? ¹²Now go; I will help you speak and will teach you what to say."

¹³But Moses said, "O LORD, please send someone else to do it."

¹⁴Then the LORD's anger burned against Moses and he said, "What about your brother, Aaron the Levite? I know he can speak well. He is already on his way to meet you, and his heart will be glad when he sees you. ¹⁵You shall speak to him and put words in his mouth; I will help both of you speak and will teach you what to do. ¹⁶He will speak to the people for you, and it will be as if he were your mouth and as if you were God to him. ¹⁷But take this staff in your hand so you can perform miraculous signs with it."

1. What do Moses' objections sound like to you?
- ❏ lazy excuses
- ❏ low self-esteem
- ❏ honest concerns
- ❏ genuine humility
- ❏ gripping fear
- ❏ daring defiance

2. If you were Moses, how would you have felt when God said he was sending you back to Egypt to lead the people of Israel out of slavery?
- ❏ scared spitless
- ❏ unwilling
- ❏ eager
- ❏ unable

3. What do you think was the point of the miraculous signs?
- ❏ God was showing off.
- ❏ God was answering Moses' objection about people not believing or listening to him.
- ❏ God was demonstrating his power to Moses.
- ❏ God was transferring his power to Moses.

4. What is the hardest thing God has asked you to do? How did you react to this?

"God does not so much need people to do extraordinary things as he needs people who do ordinary things extraordinarily well."
—William Barclay

5. Do you think Moses was more uncertain of himself or God? Who are you most uncertain of—yourself or God?

6. How would you finish this sentence? "I am committed to know and follow the will of God for my life ..."
   ❏ all of the time   ❏ some of the time
   ❏ most of the time   ❏ on occasion

7. What gifts do you believe God has given you?

8. To the extent that you are reluctant to identify and use your gifts, what would be the reason?
   ❏ lazy excuses   ❏ gripping fear
   ❏ low self-esteem   ❏ daring defiance
   ❏ honest searching and concerns ❏ other:_____
   ❏ genuine humility (lack of qualifications)
   ❏ I'm afraid I might not be hearing God correctly.
   ❏ I really don't have any reluctance.

9. What would it take for you to step out in faith and follow God's call on your life?
   ❏ a miraculous sign
   ❏ encouragement from God
   ❏ encouragement from others (like Aaron)
   ❏ God's wrath
   ❏ other:_____

Option 2 / Epistle Study

Romans 12:1–8 / Living Sacrifices

The first 11 chapters of the apostle Paul's letter to the Romans are known for their emphasis on doctrine and theology. With chapter 12, Paul shifts to practical teaching for how believers should live. Paul writes that one of the ways we can please God and strengthen the body of Christ is by knowing and using our spiritual gifts. Read Romans 12:1–8 and discuss the questions that follow with your group.

12 *Therefore, I urge you, brothers, in view of God's mercy, to offer your bodies as living sacrifices, holy and pleasing to God—this is your spiritual act of worship. ²Do not conform any longer to the pattern of this world, but be transformed by the renewing of your mind. Then you will be* *able to test and approve what God's will is—his good, pleasing and perfect will.*

³For by the grace given me I say to every one of you: Do not think of yourself more highly than you ought, but rather think of yourself with sober judgment, in accordance with the measure of faith God has given you. ⁴Just as each of us has one body with many members, and these members do not all have the same function, ⁵so in Christ we who are many form one body, and each member belongs to all the others. ⁶We have different gifts, according to the grace given us. If a man's gift is prophesying, let him use it in proportion to his faith. ⁷If it is serving, let him serve; if it is teaching, let him teach; ⁸if it is encouraging, let him encourage; if it is contributing to the needs of others, let him give generously; if it is leadership, let him govern diligently; if it is showing mercy, let him do it cheerfully.

1. What is the tradition in your family regarding opening Christmas presents? Do you receive more enjoyment from giving or receiving?

2. In the past week, did you feel more "conformed" or "transformed"?

3. What does it mean for you to offer your body as a living sacrifice to God (v. 1)?

"God has not called me to be successful; he has called me to be faithful."
—Mother Teresa

4. How can you "renew your mind" (v. 2)? What is the result if you will do so?

5. What person in your church comes to mind as someone who is really using his or her gift?

6. When it comes to viewing yourself in relation to spiritual gifts, are you inclined to "think of yourself more highly than you ought" (v. 3) or to put yourself down?

7. Transfer your scores from the Ice-Breaker at the beginning of this session to the blanks below. As you do, read the descriptions of the seven types of gifts.

    _____P = PROPHET / PERCEIVER: Truth-oriented. Forthright, outspoken, uncompromising. Open to "inspired messages" from God, and called to pray about what is perceived. Desperately needed and potentially dangerous.

    _____S = SERVER: Needs-oriented. Practical. Hard-working and conscientious. Is satisfied when things get done, regardless of who gets the credit. Can be resentful when others don't serve.

_____T = TEACHER: Concept-oriented. Systematic and logical. Has good insight into Scripture and makes things clear to others. Can be too intellectual.

_____E = ENCOURAGER / EXHORTER: Growth-oriented. Good at setting goals and motivating others. Disciplined and single-minded. Can be demanding. Hard on self and others.

_____G = GIVER: Cause-oriented. Loves to give. Able to see "big picture" and assess resources. Handles money wisely. Can be impatient with others who misuse time and/or money.

_____A = ADMINISTRATOR / LEADER: Task-oriented. Organized, decisive and thrives under pressure. Good at delegating responsibility and getting things done through others. Can be pushy.

_____C = COMPASSION / MERCY PERSON: Feeling-oriented. Highly sensitive to others in need. Compassionate and affirming. Good at listening, caring and "being present" when someone is hurting. Can get drained.

8. Which two of the gifts were your highest? Do you agree with that assessment, or do you view different gifts as your highest? (If you have time, you could see which gift(s) the others in the group would observe as your highest.)

9. What affect does this study have on how you see yourself and your gifts? Does it in any way confirm or redirect the way you function within the body of Christ?

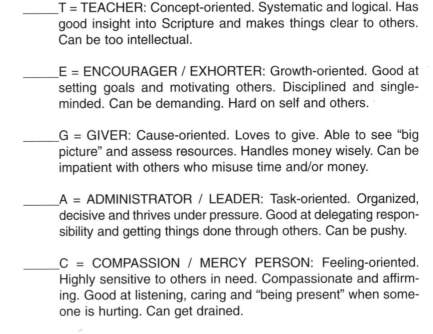

Caring Time / 15–45 Minutes

Take some time to share any personal prayer requests and answer the question:

"How do you need God's help in any struggles you're having determining your gifts or your calling?"

LEADER: Ask the group, "Who are you going to invite next week?"

Close with a short time of prayer, remembering the requests that have been shared. If you would like to pray in silence, say the word "Amen" when you have finished your prayer, so that the next person will know when to start.

Reference Notes

Summary. From doctrine Paul now turns almost by reflex to duty: how one lives flows quite naturally out of what one believes. Exposition has become exhortation.

12:1 *in view of God's mercy.* A Christian's motivation to obedience is overwhelming gratitude for God's mercy.

bodies. The Christian lifestyle is not a matter of mystical spirituality that transcends one's bodily nature, but an everyday, practical exercise of love (Romans 6:13; 13:8). The idea of "bodies" also emphasizes the metaphor of sacrifice since one puts bodies on the altar.

sacrifices. In the Old Testament sacrificial system, the victim of the sacrifice becomes wholly the property of God. Sacrifice becomes holy, i.e., set apart for God only.

living ... holy ... pleasing to God. In Greek, these three phrases are attached with equal weight as qualifiers to "sacrifices." The idea is not that God counts living sacrifices the same as the dead animals in the old system, but rather that he wants Christians to live in fullness of life, in accord with his principles (i.e., sanctification), and hence to be the kind of sacrifice desired by God.

12:2 *Do not conform.* Believers are no longer helpless victims of natural and supernatural forces which would shape them into a distorted pattern; rather they now have the ability to resist such powers.

be transformed. The force of the verb is "continue to let yourself be transformed"; i.e., a continuous action by the Holy Spirit which goes on for a lifetime. A Christian's responsibility is to stay open to this process as the Spirit works to teach them to look at life from God's view of reality.

renewing of your mind. Develop a spiritual sensitivity and perception—learn to look at life on the basis of God's view of reality. Paul emphasizes the need to develop understanding of God's ways.

test and approve. Christians are called to a responsible freedom of choice and action, based on the inner renewing work of the Holy Spirit.

12:3–8 Paul now turns to the Christian community as a whole—understanding it to be composed of believers with different gifts.

12:3 *every one of you.* The truth about spiritual gifts applies to each believer.

sober judgment. The command is to know oneself (especially one's gifts) accurately, rather than to have too high an opinion of oneself in comparison to others. This attitude enables a body of believers to blend their gifts together in harmonious ministry.

12:4–5 Using a picture that could be understood in all cultures—the body—Paul defines the nature of the Christian community: diverse gifts, but all part of one body, the body of Christ.

12:5 *each member belongs to all the others.* This is the critical insight that makes for harmony in the church. Believers must recognize that they are interdependent, needing to give to and receive from one another.

12:6 *gifts.* Those endowments given by God to every believer by grace (the words "grace" and "gifts" come from the same root word) to be used in God's service. The gifts listed here (or elsewhere) are not meant to be exhaustive or absolute since no gift list overlaps completely.

prophesying. Inspired utterances, distinguished from teaching by their immediacy and unpremeditated nature, the source of which is direct revelation by God. Prophesying was highly valued in the New Testament church (1 Cor. 14:1).

in proportion to his faith. This could mean that prophets are to resist adding their own words to the prophecy, or it could mean that they must measure their utterances in accord with "the faith"; i.e., Christian doctrine.

12:7 *serving.* The capacity for rendering practical service to the needy.

teaching. In contrast to the prophet (whose utterances have as their source the direct revelation of God), the teacher relied on the Old Testament Scriptures and the teachings of Jesus to instruct others.

12:8 Paul concludes his brief discussion of spiritual gifts with this emphasis on the fact that whatever gift one has, it should be exercised with enthusiasm for the good of others!

encouraging. This is supporting and assisting others to live a life of obedience to God.

contributing. The person who takes delight in giving away his or her possessions.

leadership. Those with special ability to guide a congregation are called upon to do so with zeal.

mercy. "The person whose special function is, on behalf of the congregation, to tend the sick, relieve the pain, or care for the aged or disabled" (Cranfield). Note that three of the seven gifts involve practical assistance to the needy.

Developing Our Gifts

3-PART AGENDA

ICE-BREAKER
15 Minutes

BIBLE STUDY
30 Minutes

CARING TIME
15–45 Minutes

The focus of the last session was on discovering your gifts. In this session, we will expand on that process. Discovering our gifts shouldn't be an end in itself. Although it is enjoyable and helpful to analyze who we are and what our gifts are, the process doesn't bear fruit unless we act on what we have learned.

It sounds obvious, but the only way we can confirm and develop our gifts is by using them. For example, if you sense that you have a gift and ability to compassionately care for sick people, then why not get plugged into your church's hospital or shut-in visitation ministry? If you feel that you score highest as a "perceiver," then why not volunteer to help coordinate your church's intercessory prayer ministry? Or if you're drawn to serving, then why not find out what practical areas of help your church needs?

It is helpful to receive the input of those who know us concerning the gifts and strengths they see in us. Fellow believers can assist us in clarifying our gifts and the best way for us to use them. Through a process, often of trial and error, we can confirm our spiritual gifts and discover what tasks we do best.

LEADER: If you have a new person at this session, remember to use Option 1 rather than Option 2 for the Bible Study. During the Caring Time, don't forget to keep praying for the empty chair.

In this session, we will look at how we can develop our gifts. In the Option 1 Study (from the book of Acts), we will look at some men who were selected to minister to the needs of others on the basis of their gifts. In the Option 2 Study (from Paul's first letter to the Corinthians), we will look at Paul's assurance that we are all given gifts by the Spirit for the common good, and that these work together like parts of a body. Take note that in the Caring Time you will have an opportunity to affirm the gifts that you see in the other members of your group.

Ice-Breaker / 15 Minutes

Child Prodigies. Look at the categories below, taking one at a time. Pick the person in your group that you think may have excelled in this area. Then have that person share how accurate the group's judgment was regarding their childhood accomplishments.

_____ smuggling stray animals into the house

_____ having (and surviving) childhood accidents

_____ talking at an early age

_____ climbing the highest trees in the neighborhood

_____ playing practical jokes

_____ having the most successful lemonade stand

_____ inventing games that the other children wanted to play

_____ taking the car on a joy ride at an early age

_____ riding the roller coaster the most times in a row

_____ breaking the most windows with baseballs

Bible Study / 30 Minutes

Option 1 / Story Passage

Acts 6:1–7 / A Division of Duties

Growing numbers of new believers led to a problem centered around questions of fairness in the distribution of food to the poor widows in the early church at Jerusalem. The "Grecian Jews" were Jews with a Greek or Hellenistic cultural background who came from outside Palestine. The "Hebraic Jews" were native to Palestine, and maintained Jewish customs and culture. Since the leaders of the church in Jerusalem were Hebraic Jews, they may have been more aware of the needs of that segment of the church. The names of the men chosen to distribute the food indicate that all seven were Grecian Jews. The complaints came from their ranks, so this would ensure that their concerns were fairly represented. Read Acts 6:1–7 and answer the questions which follow with your group.

6 *In those days when the number of disciples was increasing, the Grecian Jews among them complained against the Hebraic Jews because their widows were being overlooked in the daily distribution of food. ²So the Twelve gathered all the disciples together and said, "It would not be right for us to neglect the ministry of the word of God in order to wait on tables. ³Brothers, choose seven men from among you who are known to be full of the Spirit and wisdom. We will turn this responsibility over to them ⁴and will give our attention to prayer and the ministry of the word."*

⁵This proposal pleased the whole group. They chose Stephen, a man full of faith and of the Holy Spirit; also Philip, Procorus, Nicanor, Timon, Parmenas, and Nicolas from Antioch, a convert to Judaism. ⁶They presented these men to the apostles, who prayed and laid their hands on them.

⁷So the word of God spread. The number of disciples in Jerusalem increased rapidly, and a large number of priests became obedient to the faith.

"Work is love made visible. And if you cannot work with love, but only with distaste, it is better that you should leave your work and sit at the gate of the temple and take alms of those who work with joy."
—Kahil Gibran

1. If you were one of the Twelve and heard this complaint by the Grecian Jews, what would have been your first response?
- ❏ Sounds like little kids: "She's getting more than I am!"
- ❏ What do they expect from us? We're doing so much already.
- ❏ I'm glad they felt comfortable telling us about this.
- ❏ You have to expect conflict when you are growing fast.
- ❏ If people are in need, we must respond quickly.

2. In verse 2, the Twelve said, "It would not be right for us to neglect the ministry of the word of God in order to wait on tables." How do you respond to their statement?
- ❏ It sounds like they were too good for that.
- ❏ They were so excited about what they were doing, they didn't want to interrupt it.
- ❏ They realized the number of things that needed to be done were more than they could handle without additional help.
- ❏ They knew what their gifts and calling were.
- ❏ other:_____

3. How would you feel if you were one of the seven persons selected for this task?
- ❏ used—to have to do the dirty work that others didn't want to do
- ❏ useful—that my life would really help others
- ❏ imposed upon—another "committee assignment"
- ❏ honored—especially since the apostles were looking for individuals "known to be full of the Spirit and wisdom"
- ❏ angry—that it didn't seem like I had a choice in the matter

4. What is the significance of the fact that these men—rather than volunteering—were chosen for the job?
   ❏ It shows that the early church was autocratic.
   ❏ Others often recognize our gifts more easily than we do.
   ❏ Probably no one would have volunteered for such a job.
   ❏ Volunteers may not have been suited to the job.
   ❏ It got the whole church involved in the process.

5. Place an *"X"* on the line below to indicate which of the two statements you agree with more:

   _____

   All gifts are of equal   Some gifts have greater value
   value and dignity.   and dignity than others.

6. What do you feel is the most important variable in whether or not you are able to find purpose in what you're doing in life?
   ❏ believing in God's direction
   ❏ knowing myself and my gifts and talents
   ❏ the ability to focus on something other than self
   ❏ flexibility of thinking—being able to find purpose in the smallest task
   ❏ willingness to think about purpose instead of money and status
   ❏ not being too philosophical—The purpose of life is survival!

7. What job or task have you been selected to do where you were proud of being chosen? (It can be at work, at church, or in your community.) What gifts were required for you to do this task?

8. What job or task have you been asked to do where you were embarrassed or disgusted about being selected? (It can be at work, at church, in your community, or in your home.) After studying this passage, do you feel differently about that task?
   ❏ Yes—I can see where I was used by God even in that task.
   ❏ Maybe—but the task was still degrading.
   ❏ No—the task was beneath anyone.
   ❏ No—and I don't want to view that horrible task any differently.
   ❏ other:_____

9. What abilities or spiritual gifts have other people identified in your life? How could you use those gifts more than you do?

Leadership Training Supplement

YOU ARE
HERE

BIRTH	GROWTH	RELEASE

101

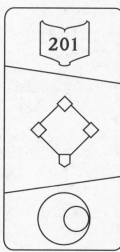

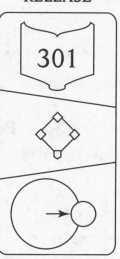

201

301

What is the game plan for your group in the 101 stage?

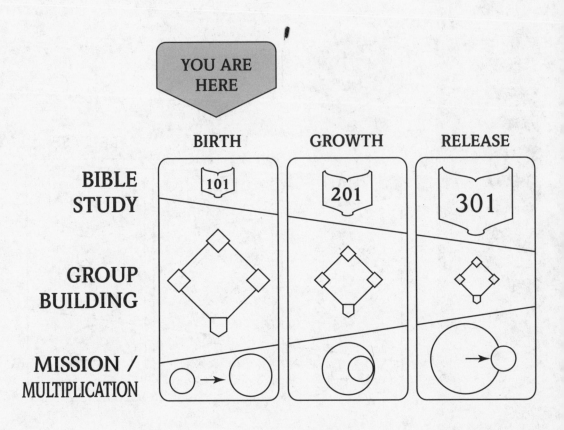

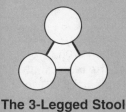

The 3-Legged Stool

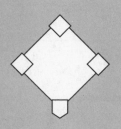

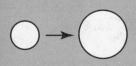

The three essentials in a healthy small group are Bible Study, Group Building and Mission / Multiplication. You need all three to stay balanced—like a 3-legged stool.
- To focus only on Bible Study will lead to scholasticism.
- To focus only on Group Building will lead to narcissism.
- To focus only on Mission will lead to burnout.

You need a game plan for the life cycle of the group where all three of these elements are present in a mission-driven strategy. In the first stage of the group, here is the game plan:

Bible Study

To share your spiritual story through Scripture.

The greatest gift you can give a group is the gift of your spiritual story—the story of your spiritual beginnings, your spiritual growing pains, struggles, hopes and fears. The Bible Study is designed to help you tell your spiritual story to the group.

Group Building

To become a caring community.

In the first stage of a group, note how the baseball diamond is larger than the book and the circles. This is because Group Building is the priority in the first stage. Group Building is a four-step process to become a close-knit group. Using the baseball diamond illustration, the goal of Group Building—bonding—is home plate. But to get there you have to go around the bases.

Mission / Multiplication

To grow your group numerically and spiritually.

The mission of your group is the greatest mission anyone can give their life to—to bring new people into a personal relationship with Christ and the fellowship of a Christian community. This purpose will become more prominent in the second and third stages of your group. In this stage, the goal is to invite new people into your group and try to double.

Bible Study

In the first stage of a group, the Bible Study is where you get to know each other and share your spiritual stories. The Bible Study is designed to give the leader the option of going LIGHT or HEAVY, depending on the background of the people in the group. OPTION 1 is especially designed for beginner groups who do not know a lot about the Bible or each other. OPTION 2 is for groups who are familiar with the Bible and with one another.

Option 1   Relational Bible Study (Stories)

Designed around a guided questionnaire, the questions move across the Disclosure Scale from "no risk" questions about people in the Bible story to "high risk" questions about your own life and how you would react in that situation. "If you had been in the story ..." or "The person in the story like me is ... " The questions are open-ended—with multiple-choice options and no right or wrong answers. A person with no background knowledge of the Bible may actually have the advantage because the questions are based on first impressions.

The STORY	GUIDED QUESTIONNAIRE	My STORY
in Scripture	1 2 3 4 5 6 7 8	compared

OPTION 1: Light RELATIONAL BIBLE STUDY	OPTION 2: Heavy INDUCTIVE BIBLE STUDY
• Based on Bible stories • Open-ended questions • To share your spiritual story	• Based on Bible teachings • With observation questions • To dig into Scripture

Option 2   Inductive Bible Study (Teachings)

For groups who know each other, OPTION 2 gives you the choice to go deeper in Bible Study, with questions about the text on three levels:

- Observation: What is the text saying?
- Interpretation: What does it mean?
- Application: What are you going to do about it?

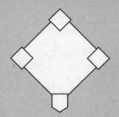

Group Building

The Baseball Diamond illustrates the four-step sharing process in bonding to become a group: (1) input; (2) feedback; (3) deeper input; and (4) deeper feedback. This process is carefully structured into the seven sessions of this course, as follows:

 Sharing My Story. My religious background. My early years and where I am right now in my spiritual journey.

 Affirming Each Other's Story. "Thank you for sharing ..." "Your story became a gift to me ..." "Your story helps me to understand where you are coming from ..."

 Sharing My Needs. "This is where I'm struggling and hurting. This is where I need to go—what I need to do."

 Caring for One Another. "How can we help you in prayer this week?" Ministry occurs as the group members serve one another through the Holy Spirit.

Mission / Multiplication

To prove that your group is "Mission-Driven," now is the time to start praying for your new "baby"—a new group to be born in the future. This is the MISSION of your group.

The birthing process begins by growing your group to about 10 or 12 people. Here are three suggestions to help your group stay focused on your Mission:

1. **Empty Chair.** Pull up an empty chair at the Caring Time and ask God to fill this chair at the next meeting.

2. **Refrigerator List.** Jot down the names of people you are going to invite and put this list on the refrigerator.

3. **New Member Home.** Move to the home of the newest member—where their friends will feel comfortable when they come to the group. On the next page, some of your questions about bringing new people into your group are answered.

Leadership Training

What if a new person joins the group in the third or fourth session?

Call the "Option Play" and go back to an OPTION 1 Bible Study that allows this person to "share their story" and get to know the people in the group.

What do you do when the group gets too large for sharing?

Take advantage of the three-part agenda and subdivide into groups of four for the Bible Study time. Count off around the group: "one, two, one, two"—and have the "ones" move quickly to another room for sharing.

What is the long-term expectation of the group for mission?

To grow the size of the group and eventually start a new group after one or two years.

What do you do when the group does not want to multiply?

This is the reason why this MISSION needs to be discussed at the beginning of a group—not at the end. If the group is committed to this MISSION at the outset, and works on this mission in stage one, they will be ready for multiplication at the end of the final stage.

What are the principles behind the Serendipity approach to Bible Study for a beginner group?

1. *Level the Playing Field.* Start the sharing with things that are easy to talk about and where everyone is equal—things that are instantly recallable—light, mischievously revealing and childlike. Meet at the human side before moving into spiritual things.

2. *Share Your Spiritual Story.* Group Building, especially for new groups, is essential. It is crucial for Bible Study in beginner groups to help the group become a community by giving everyone the opportunity to share their spiritual history.

3. *Open Questions / Right Brain.* Open-ended questions are better than closed questions. Open questions allow for options, observations and a variety of opinions in which no one is right or wrong. Similarly, "right-brained" questions are

better than "left-brained" questions. Right-brained questions seek out your first impressions, tone, motives and subjective feelings about the text. Right-brained questions work well with narratives. Multiple-choice questionnaires encourage people who know very little about the Bible. Given a set of multiple-choice options, a new believer is not threatened, and a shy person is not intimidated. Everyone has something to contribute.

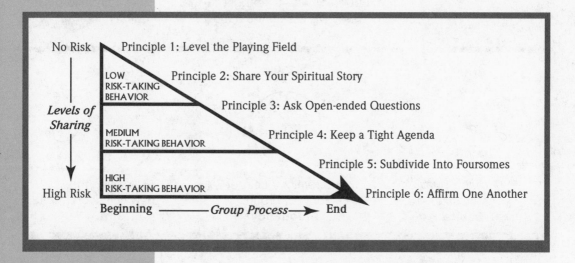

4. Tight Agenda. A tight agenda is better than a loose agenda for beginning small groups. Those people who might be nervous about "sharing" will find comfort knowing that the meeting agenda has been carefully organized. The more structure the first few meetings have the better, especially for a new group. Some people are afraid that a structured agenda will limit discussion. In fact, the opposite is true. The Serendipity agenda is designed to keep the discussion focused on what's important and to bring out genuine feelings, issues, and areas of need. If the goal is to move the group toward deeper relationships and a deeper experience of God, then a structured agenda is the best way to achieve that goal.

5. Fearless Foursomes. Dividing your small group into foursomes during the Bible Study can be a good idea. In groups of four, everyone will have an opportunity to participate and you can finish the Bible Study in 30 minutes. In groups of eight or more, the Bible Study will need to be longer and you will take away from the Caring Time.

Leadership Training

Also, by subdividing into groups of four for the Bible Study time, you give others a chance to develop their skills at leading a group—in preparation for the day when you develop a small cell to eventually move out and birth a new group.

6. *Affirm the person and their story.* Give positive feedback to group members: "Thank you for sharing ... " "Your story really helps me to understand where you are coming from ... " "Your story was a real gift to me ... " This affirmation given honestly will create the atmosphere for deeper sharing.

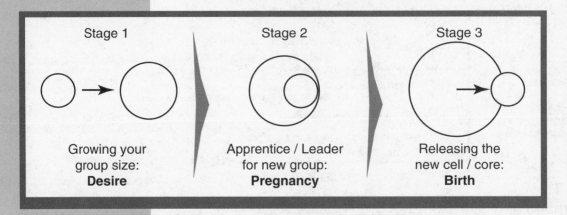

Stage 1	Stage 2	Stage 3
Growing your group size: **Desire**	Apprentice / Leader for new group: **Pregnancy**	Releasing the new cell / core: **Birth**

What is the next stage of our group all about?

In the next stage, the 201 BIBLE STUDY is deeper, GROUP BUILDING focuses on developing your gifts, and in the MISSION you will identify an Apprentice / Leader and two others within your group who will eventually become the leadership core of a new group down the road a bit.

Option 2 / Epistle Study

1 Corinthians 12:7–27 / A Variety of Gifts

Paul wrote the following passage because some Christians at Corinth apparently felt that everyone should be the same and have the same gift. This attitude was causing division in the church. So Paul wrote to tell them that no gifts are inferior and that all are necessary in the body of Christ. Read 1 Corinthians 12:7–27 and discuss the questions which follow with your group.

7Now to each one the manifestation of the Spirit is given for the common good. 8To one there is given through the Spirit the message of wisdom, to another the message of knowledge by means of the same Spirit, 9to another faith by the same Spirit, to another gifts of healing by that one Spirit, 10to another miraculous powers, to another prophecy, to another distinguishing between spirits, to another speaking in different kinds of tongues, and to still another the interpretation of tongues. 11All these are the work of one and the same Spirit, and he gives them to each one, just as he determines.

12The body is a unit, though it is made up of many parts; and though all its parts are many, they form one body. So it is with Christ. 13For we were all baptized by one Spirit into one body—whether Jews or Greeks, slave or free—and we were all given the one Spirit to drink.

14Now the body is not made up of one part but of many. 15If the foot should say, "Because I am not a hand, I do not belong to the body," it would not for that reason cease to be part of the body. 16And if the ear should say, "Because I am not an eye, I do not belong to the body," it would not for that reason cease to be part of the body. 17If the whole body were an eye, where would the sense of hearing be? If the whole body were an ear, where would the sense of smell be? 18But in fact God has arranged the parts in the body, every one of them, just as he wanted them to be. 19If they were all one part, where would the body be? 20As it is, there are many parts, but one body.

21The eye cannot say to the hand, "I don't need you!" And the head cannot say to the feet, "I don't need you!" 22On the contrary, those parts of the body that seem to be weaker are indispensable, 23and the parts that we think are less honorable we treat with special honor. And the parts that are unpresentable are treated with special modesty, 24while our presentable parts need no special treatment. But God has combined the members of the body and has given greater honor to the parts that lacked it, 25so that there should be no division in the body, but that its parts should have equal concern for each other. 26If one part suffers, every part suffers with it; if one part is honored, every part rejoices with it.

27Now you are the body of Christ, and each one of you is a part of it.

1. When have you felt that you were part of a unit where all the parts worked together for a common goal?

2. What truths about spiritual gifts are emphasized in verses 7 and 11?

3. What attitudes have you encountered toward spiritual gifts? Spiritual gifts are for:
   ❏ ministers only
   ❏ religious fanatics
   ❏ the more spiritually mature
   ❏ all believers
   ❏ the first-century church only
   ❏ believers who have had a special experience
   ❏ other:_____

4. In verses 12–13, in what ways does Paul stress the unity of believers?

5. Which parts of the body do you identify with the most?
   ❏ a foot—I'll go anywhere to serve God.
   ❏ a hand—I like to help out.
   ❏ an ear—I'm a good listener.
   ❏ an eye—I can see what needs to be done.
   ❏ a leg—I keep things moving.
   ❏ the head—I'm fulfilled by leading or organizing.
   ❏ the mouth—I express myself well.

6. How does this passage make you feel about your place in the body of Christ? About your need for others?

7. What does the church need to do better to be the kind of unit where everyone knows they have a part and they are developing their gifts?
   ❏ rely more on the Spirit
   ❏ be more accepting of diversity
   ❏ be more aware of the gifts people have
   ❏ be more affirming, especially of the less glamorous gifts
   ❏ provide more training so people can develop their gifts
   ❏ support each other more (suffering and rejoicing with one another)
   ❏ other:_____

8. How connected are you to your church body? What could you do to be more connected?

9. How do you (or could you) use your gifts within the church, Christ's body? What holds you back from using your gifts more fully?

"Though one person may have a more responsible position, in God's sight even the person who may go unnoticed is just as important and necessary in the body of Christ."
—Gene Getz

Caring Time / 15–45 Minutes

Go around the group and have one person at a time listen while others affirm the "gifts" (spiritual gifts, talents, abilities) they see in that person (and perhaps how they have observed those gifts functioning).

Thank God for the gifts of the members of the group, and pray for God's guidance in using those gifts in a way that pleases him.

Reference Notes

Summary. In chapters 12–14, Paul deals with the third and final issue related to the worship experience of the Corinthian church: the abuse of the gift of tongues. His emphasis here is on the variety of gifts given by the Spirit, over against the Corinthians' preoccupation with one particular gift.

12:7 *to each one.* Every Christian has a spiritual gift.

for the common good. The purpose of these gifts is not private advantage, but community growth.

12:8 *wisdom / knowledge.* It is not clear how (or if) these gifts differ. Perhaps a message of wisdom focused on practical, ethical instruction, while a message of knowledge involved exposition of biblical truth.

12:9 *faith.* Special ability "to claim from God extraordinary manifestations of power in the natural world" (Barrett). Saving faith, which all Christians share, is not in view here.

healing. Special ability to effect miraculous cures. Paul apparently had this gift (Acts 14:8–10).

12:10 *miraculous powers.* Probably the gift of exorcism and similar types of confrontation with evil supernatural powers.

prophecy. Inspired utterances given in ordinary (not ecstatic) speech, distinguished from teaching and wisdom by its unpremeditated nature.

distinguishing between spirits. Just because a person claimed to be inspired by the Holy Spirit did not make it true. Those who possessed this gift of discernment were able to identify the source of an utterance—whether it came from the Holy Spirit or another spirit.

tongues. Ecstatic speech, unintelligible except by those with the gift of interpretation of tongues.

12:12–27 Having pointed out the diversity of gifts in 12:1–11, now Paul examines the unity that exists within all this diversity. Once having established that Christians are all part of one body (vv. 12–13), Paul returns then to the idea of diversity, in which he not only points out the variety of gifts that exist, but the fact that none are inferior and all are necessary.

12:12 *a unit ... made up of many parts.* This is Paul's central point in verses 12–30: "diversity within unity (Fee)."

So it is with Christ. The church is the body of Christ (v. 27), and so indeed Christ can be understood to be made up of many parts. Yet he is also the Lord (12:3), and thus head over that church.

12:13 Here Paul points to the unity side of the body of Christ. Unity exists because all were baptized into one Spirit, and all drink from one Spirit. His concern is not with how people become believers, but with how believers become one body. The term "baptism" is probably metaphorical (Fee). The way believers are "put into one Spirit" is like baptism; i.e., "think of it as being immersed in the Spirit."

baptized by one Spirit. In fact, the footnoted translation of the preposition in the New International Version is probably the correct rendering: "baptized in one Spirit," since Paul's concern is not with the means by which believers are baptized, but with the common reality in which all believers exist; i.e., the Holy Spirit (Fee).

one Spirit to drink. Paul continues speaking metaphorically, with the idea of water still dominant. Being incorporated into one body is not only like baptism, it is also like "drinking the same Spirit."

12:14 Now Paul points to the diversity side of the body of Christ (which is his major concern): the one body has many different parts to it.

12:15–26 Having established that all Christians are part of one body (which is, in fact, Christ's body) and that this body has a variety of parts, Paul then develops an elaborate metaphor based on the human body. He makes two points: There are a variety of gifts (vv. 15–20), and each gift is vital, regardless of its nature (vv. 21–26).

12:15–20 It is just as ludicrous for Christians to opt out of the body of Christ (presumably by not using their gifts during worship) because they have one gift and not another (presumably more desired) gift, as it is for a foot (or ear) to decide not to be a part of a physical body because it is not a hand (or eye).

12:21–26 Just as it is presumptuous of the eye (or head) to say to the hand (or foot) that it has no need of it, so too, a Christian ought not to deny the value, need or function of anyone's spiritual gift, especially on the basis that it is different from (or inferior to) one's own gift.

12:21 Each part of the body needs the other parts. No one gift (e.g., tongues) can stand alone. Wholeness in the body requires that all the parts function together.

12:22 *weaker.* "The delicate organs, such as the eye; and the invisible organs such as the heart" (Barrett).

12:26 In fact, the whole person suffers when one (to use a modern example) sprains an ankle. It is not just the ankle that suffers.

12:27 Paul sums up the meaning of his metaphor.

the body of Christ. By this phrase, Paul conveys the idea not that Christ consists of this body, but that Christ rules over this body, and that this body belongs to him.

Taking Risks

3-PART AGENDA

ICE-BREAKER
15 Minutes

BIBLE STUDY
30 Minutes

CARING TIME
15–45 Minutes

In an ideal world, everyone would be absolutely sure what their calling was and what their gifts were. And everyone would know that using those gifts in their calling would lead to fulfillment and satisfaction. However, this is not an ideal world. So, for instance, when we are in one job (and strongly suspect that our true calling is in another area), we may have to risk switching jobs, even though we are not 100% sure. We might risk giving up a secure job with a steady income for an uncertain job with less pay. Finding and following our calling—whether in our career or in our role in the body of Christ—involves taking risks.

LEADER: If you haven't already, now is the time to start thinking about the next step for your group. Take a look at the 201 courses (the second stage in the small group life cycle) on the inside of the back cover.

To say that taking risks is necessary to find our calling is not to say that all such venturing is bad. Actually, having to risk can be part of life's excitement. Author Bruce Larson (in his book *There's a Lot More to Health Than Not Being Sick*) writes what his physician told him when he reached middle age: "Middle age is a time when people are advised to take it easy. You start to live very cautiously. You avoid anything new or risky and you end up hastening the whole aging process." Risk can add to the excitement of life. And that can actually make us healthier! Larson goes on to discuss God's role in this, writing: "I acknowledge that risk for risk's sake, while it may be healthier, is not very productive. But God seems to be calling us to a life of creative risk. We are to be those people who are prayerfully seeking to bring about God's will and way in the affairs of men and who can give themselves to those causes with abandon."

Creative risk—it is a vital ingredient in finding and living out our call. This session will help us see what it means to risk as we search for that call. In Option 1, we will look at the Parable of the Talents (Matthew 25:14–30). In it, we will consider how Jesus commended the servants who took some risks to invest in the kingdom. In Option 2 (2 Timothy 1:3–14), we will examine Paul's advice to young Timothy that he not approach life with timidity.

Ice-Breaker / 15 Minutes

My Risk Quotient. This test is a fun way to figure out how much of a risk-taker you are. Go through the questions one at a time, circling the appropriate letter and having everyone share their answers. Then figure out your score and share your results.

1. In playing Monopoly, I usually:
   a. play it safe / stash my cash
   b. stay cool and hold back a little
   c. go for broke—gambling everything

2. In choosing a job, I would prefer:
   a. a boring job with security
   b. an interesting job with some security
   c. starting my own company with no security

3. On a menu, I usually pick:
   a. something familiar that I know I like
   b. something that's a little different
   c. something way-out that I've never tried

4. At a party, I usually:
   a. stick with my friends
   b. reach out to one stranger
   c. see how many new people I can meet

5. In starting a relationship, I usually:
   a. let the other person do the talking
   b. meet the other person halfway
   c. take the initiative

6. I would prefer my life to have:
   a. no risks and lots of safety
   b. some risks and some safety
   c. lots of risk and little safety

Scoring: Give yourself 1 point for every "a," 2 points for every "b," and 3 points for every "c." Then circle the total on the line below to get your risk quotient.

PLAY IT SAFE　　　　　　　　　　　　　　　　　　　　**TAKE A CHANCE**

6	7	8	9	10	11	12	13	14	15	16	17	18

Bible Study / 30 Minutes

Option 1 / Gospel Study

Matthew 25:14–30 / The Risk of Investment

The following parable is one of many that Jesus told to clarify our role in doing the work of the kingdom of God. The term "talent" was first used for a unit of coins. The present-day use of "talent" as an ability comes from this parable. Read Matthew 25:14–30 and discuss the questions which follow with your group.

14"Again, it will be like a man going on a journey, who called his servants and entrusted his property to them. 15To one he gave five talents of money, to another two talents, and to another one talent, each according to his ability. Then he went on his journey. 16The man who had received the five talents went at once and put his money to work and gained five more. 17So also, the one with the two talents gained two more. 18But the man who had received the one talent went off, dug a hole in the ground and hid his master's money.

19"After a long time the master of those servants returned and settled accounts with them. 20The man who had received the five talents brought the other five. 'Master,' he said, 'you entrusted me with five talents. See, I have gained five more.'

21"His master replied, 'Well done, good and faithful servant! You have been faithful with a few things; I will put you in charge of many things. Come and share your master's happiness!'

22"The man with the two talents also came. 'Master,' he said, 'you entrusted me with two talents; see, I have gained two more.'

23"His master replied, 'Well done, good and faithful servant! You have been faithful with a few things; I will put you in charge of many things. Come and share your master's happiness!'

24"Then the man who had received the one talent came. 'Master,' he said, 'I knew that you are a hard man, harvesting where you have not sown and gathering where you have not scattered seed. 25So I was afraid and went out and hid your talent in the ground. See, here is what belongs to you.'

26"His master replied, 'You wicked, lazy servant! So you knew that I harvest where I have not sown and gather where I have not scattered seed? 27Well then, you should have put my money on deposit with the bankers, so that when I returned I would have received it back with interest.

28" 'Take the talent from him and give it to the one who has the ten talents. 29For everyone who has will be given more, and he will have an abundance. Whoever does not have, even what he has will be taken from him. 30And throw that worthless servant outside, into the darkness, where there will be weeping and gnashing of teeth.' "

1. Why do you think the servant given one talent hid his money?
   ❏ He was afraid of his master.
   ❏ He was afraid to take risks.
   ❏ He didn't know what to do.
   ❏ He was lazy and irresponsible.
   ❏ He resented the way the master made his money.
   ❏ He didn't know the consequences of his actions were going to be so bad.

2. What was the master saying to the two who doubled their money?
   ❏ "I'm proud of you."
   ❏ "Enter into a life of ease."
   ❏ "My investment in you paid off."
   ❏ "You'll get your reward in heaven."
   ❏ "I can trust you with bigger things."

3. What is this parable saying to you?
   ❏ God cannot tolerate laziness.
   ❏ God has given Christians a "job" to do until he returns.
   ❏ When we use what God has given us for him, God gives us more.
   ❏ Faithfulness to God requires taking risks.
   ❏ Judgment awaits those who don't invest their lives in God's kingdom.

4. Which of the following risks did you take as a child or adolescent?
   ❏ participating in "dangerous" sports
   ❏ asking someone out when I wasn't sure he or she liked me
   ❏ skipping school
   ❏ driving crazily
   ❏ working on a hazardous science project
   ❏ climbing trees, rock formations, rappelling, etc.
   ❏ trying out for exclusive groups (like cheerleader, concert choir)
   ❏ other:_____

5. How do you differentiate between healthy risk-taking and foolhardy risk-taking?

6. Write two of the talents you have discovered or which others have said you have. Then assign each talent a number (from the scale below) according to how well you're using that talent right now:

1	2	3	4	5	6	7	8	9	10
burying it									fully invested

   talent #1:_____ usage:_____
   talent #2:_____ usage:_____

7. What motivates you to use your time, resources and abilities for God's kingdom?
   ❑ fear of the Master
   ❑ people's appreciation
   ❑ God's approval
   ❑ a chance for greater responsibility
   ❑ fellowship with the Master
   ❑ rewards in the next life
   ❑ doing the best I can with the abilities God has given me
   ❑ other:_____

8. Which of the following statements describes how you feel about the way you are currently "investing" your life?
   ❑ I am quite satisfied.
   ❑ I would like to make some changes.
   ❑ I need to change, but don't know what to do.
   ❑ I'm not sure what it means to invest my life.
   ❑ I'm not doing a very good job of investing my life.
   ❑ I feel like I'm on hold.

9. What changes would be necessary in order for you to be more satisfied with your life's investment?
   ❑ get into a vocation that more fully utilizes my talents
   ❑ use my talents in my current vocation more than I do
   ❑ find ways to use my talents in a volunteer capacity
   ❑ risk using some talents I have been afraid to use
   ❑ stop worrying about failure and try *something*
   ❑ I'm already investing my talents pretty well.
   ❑ other:_____

Option 2 / Epistle Study

2 Timothy 1:3–14 / No More Timidity

The following passage was written to Timothy, a young leader in the church who Paul took under his wing. It is a personal word of encouragement to Timothy to be faithful. Read 2 Timothy 1:3–14, and discuss the questions which follow with your group.

³I thank God, whom I serve, as my forefathers did, with a clear conscience, as night and day I constantly remember you in my prayers. ⁴Recalling your tears, I long to see you, so that I may be filled with joy. ⁵I have been reminded of your sincere faith, which first lived in your grand-mother Lois and in your mother Eunice and, I am persuaded, now lives in you also. *For this reason I remind you to fan into flame the gift of God, which is in you through the laying on of my hands. *For God did not give us a spirit of timidity, but a spirit of power, of love and of self-discipline.

*So do not be ashamed to testify about our Lord, or ashamed of me his prisoner. But join with me in suffering for the gospel, by the power of God, *who has saved us and called us to a holy life—not because of anything we have done but because of his own purpose and grace. This grace was given us in Christ Jesus before the beginning of time, *but it has now been revealed through the appearing of our Savior, Christ Jesus, who has destroyed death and has brought life and immortality to light through the gospel. *And of this gospel I was appointed a herald and an apostle and a teacher. *That is why I am suffering as I am. Yet I am not ashamed, because I know whom I have believed, and am convinced that he is able to guard what I have entrusted to him for that day.

*What you heard from me, keep as the pattern of sound teaching, with faith and love in Christ Jesus. *Guard the good deposit that was entrusted to you—guard it with the help of the Holy Spirit who lives in us.

1. Who were the people in your life who—like Timothy's mother and grandmother—inspired you to faith? Who has been a mentor to you (like Paul was to Timothy)?

2. What is one weakness that Timothy has and what does Paul remind him of regarding it (see note on v. 7)?

3. What did Paul mean when he said, "God did not give us a spirit of timidity"?
❑ It's wrong to be shy.
❑ God wants us to be bold risk-takers.
❑ God doesn't want us to be held back by our fears.
❑ God doesn't want us to be ashamed of our faith.
❑ It's okay to be timid in personality, but it's a barrier to using your spiritual gifts.

4. What pressures might pull at Timothy to be ashamed of the Gospel or of Paul (see first two notes on v. 8)?

5. What kept Paul from being ashamed himself (v. 12)? What keeps you from being ashamed of the Gospel?

6. On a scale of 1 (timid) to 10 (bold), how has your Christian witness been lately?

"I will consider my earthly existence to have been wasted unless I can recall a loving family, a consistent investment in the lives of people, and an earnest attempt to serve the God who made me."
—James Dobson

7. What do you need to do to "fan into flame the gift of God" within you?
- ❏ be more in touch with the Holy Spirit
- ❏ have more courage to take risks
- ❏ get more training to develop my gifts
- ❏ use my gifts more in serving God and others
- ❏ get more encouragement from others in the use of my gifts
- ❏ other:_____

8. If Paul wrote you a letter, what would he remind you about?
- ❏ my spiritual heritage
- ❏ the sincerity and level of my faith in past times
- ❏ my spiritual mentor's influence
- ❏ the spiritual gifts God has given me
- ❏ inner power, love, and self-discipline rather than timidity or shame
- ❏ other:_____

9. Imagine that you put aside any "spirit of timidity" and acted in a "spirit of power, of love and of self-discipline." What difference would that make in how you use your gifts in service to God and others?

Caring Time / 15–45 Minutes

Take time at the close to share any personal prayer requests. Answer the question:

"How can we help you in prayer this week?"

LEADER:
Ask the group, "Who are you going to invite next week?"

Then go around and let each person pray for the person on their right. Finish the sentence,

"Dear God, I want to speak to you about my friend _____."

As you close, include a prayer for the bonding of your group members, as well as for the numerical growth of the group.

Reference Notes

Summary. Paul reminds Timothy of the gift of God within him, and urges him not to use it timidly. Rather, he is to use it with the spirit of power, love, and self-control which God has given. This especially means to be unashamed of witnessing for Christ.

1:3 *as my forefathers did.* Paul also stands squarely in the Old Testament tradition of faith of his forebearers (in contrast to the false teachers who had, effectively, left the faith).

I constantly remember you. Paul prayed regularly, and in those prayers he always remembered Timothy.

1:4 *Recalling your tears.* Paul is probably remembering when they parted the last time, he to go on to Macedonia while Timothy stayed in Ephesus (see Acts 20:37 for a similar situation).

1:5 *Eunice.* Timothy's mother was a Jewish Christian (see Acts 16:1). His father was a Gentile, who probably was not a believer.

1:6 *fan into flame.* "Rekindle." Paul uses the image of a fire, not to suggest that the gift of ministry has "gone out," but that it needs constant stirring up so that it always burns brightly.

the gift of God. Paul reminds Timothy not only of his spiritual roots (the faith of his mother and grandmother), but of the charismatic gift (*charisma* in Greek) he has been given for ministry.

1:7 Paul makes this appeal because Timothy is not a forceful person.

timidity. "The translation 'timid' is probably too weak. The word, often appearing in battle contexts, suggest 'cowardice' …" (Fee).

power / love / self-discipline. The gift the Spirit gave Timothy leads not to "timidity," but to these positive characteristics.

1:8–12 Paul's first appeal, which is found in these verses, is that Timothy remain loyal to Christ and to Paul. Timothy is able to do this because he has been given power, love and self-discipline (v. 7).

1:8 *ashamed to testify about our Lord.* The Gospel message about a dying Savior was not immediately popular in the first-century world. The Greeks laughed at the idea that the Messiah could be a convicted criminal, and that God was so weak that he would allow his own Son to die. And the Jews could not conceive of a Messiah (whom they knew to be all-powerful) dying on a cross (which they felt disqualified him from acceptance by God). It was not easy to preach the Gospel in the face of such scorn.

ashamed of me. When Paul was rearrested, his friends deserted him (see 1:15). He does not want Timothy to do the same.

his prisoner. Paul may be in a Roman jail, but he knows that he is not a prisoner of Caesar. He is, and has long been, a willing prisoner of Jesus (see Eph. 3:1; 4:1; Philemon 1,9).

join with me. In fact, rather than being ashamed of the Gospel (or of Paul and his suffering), Timothy ought to share in this suffering.

suffering. Paul understands from his own experience (and from that of Jesus) that suffering is part of what it means to follow the Gospel (see 3:12; Rom. 8:17; 2 Cor. 4:7–15; Phil. 1:12, 29; Col. 1:24; 1 Thess. 1:6).

1:9–10 Paul reminds Timothy of the *content* of the Gospel. The glorious nature of the Gospel will bolster Timothy's confidence and will give him a strong reason not to be ashamed of it.

1:9 has saved us. Timothy can face suffering because he has already experienced salvation. This is an accomplished fact.

grace. God's work of salvation depends wholly on "grace" (his unmerited favor lavished on his creation), not on "anything we have done." This grace, which was in place from "the beginning of time," is "given us in Christ Jesus" (see Eph. 1:4).

1:10 appearing. The Greek word is *epiphaneia* (from which the English word "epiphany" is derived). It refers here to the "manifestation" of God's grace via the incarnation of Christ.

Savior. This was a common title in the first century. It was applied to the Roman emperor (in his role as head of the state religion) and to various redeemer-gods in the mystery religions. Christians came to see that Jesus was the one and only Savior.

death / life. Jesus' work of salvation is described in his twofold act of destroying the power of death over people (death no longer has the final word) and bringing resurrection life in its place.

1:11–12 It is for the sake of the Gospel that Paul is now in prison—a further reason why Timothy ought not to be ashamed of him.

1:11 herald / apostle / teacher. "The apostles formulated the gospel, preachers proclaim it like heralds, and teachers instruct people systematically in its doctrines and in its ethical implications" (Stott).

1:12 I am not ashamed. The fact that he is in prison brings no shame to Paul, despite how others might view it.

6

Reflecting on Work

3-PART AGENDA

ICE-BREAKER
15 Minutes

BIBLE STUDY
30 Minutes

CARING TIME
15–45 Minutes

Finding our calling is integrally related to our attitude toward work. For some people, work is a necessary evil. They dream of the day when they will win the lottery and won't have to work anymore. Work done with that kind of attitude is particularly wearying, and is often of poor quality.

Richard Nelson Bolles—author of the book on job hunting, *What Color Is Your Parachute?*—says that our enthusiasm for doing something, and for using the gift (or gifts) we have been given, are more important aspects in discovering our "call" and "mission." We don't need more people in the world drawing a paycheck and living for the weekend. Instead, "what the world does need is more people who feel true enthusiasm for their work. People who have taken the time to think—that is, to think out what they uniquely can do, and what they uniquely have to offer the world."

To find God's will for our lives is to believe there is some work we can do with pleasure and satisfaction, because we enjoy what we are contributing. It is to believe that when we follow God's leading (in terms of life vocation), God will not lead us to work that makes us miserable. Instead, God will lead us to a job, a ministry, or to family responsibilities which makes us fulfilled and whole as persons. Thus, having a positive attitude toward the work we do derives from believing we are called to do that work. And believing we are called to do our work requires faith in God, and God's leading in our lives.

> **LEADER: This is the next to last session in this course. At the end of the course, how would you like to celebrate your time together? With a dinner? With a party? With a commitment to continue as a group?**

In this session, we will look at our attitude toward work and its relation to our gifts and calling. In the Option 1 Study (from Matthew's Gospel), we will look at a parable Jesus told about some workers who felt they were treated unfairly. In the Option 2 Study (from James' letter), we will consider what perspective we should have about our future planning.

Ice-Breaker / 15 Minutes

Our Un-Calling. To recognize our calling, perhaps it might help to eliminate some lines of work we would not like to do. We can refer to this as our "un-calling"! Look over the list below and choose the three WORST jobs. Share your choices with the group.

- ❏ crowd-control officer at a rock concert
- ❏ valet driver for the Sturgis bike rally
- ❏ food taster for an experimental organic vegetable plant
- ❏ maintenance person in charge of cleanup (including restrooms) after the Super Bowl
- ❏ public relations manager for Dennis Rodman
- ❏ teacher's aide in charge of biology department dissection lab
- ❏ manager of a local McDonald's, with 153 teenage employees
- ❏ bodyguard for Rush Limbaugh speaking at a feminist convention
- ❏ field trip supervisor for a class of 30 six-year olds visiting a museum
- ❏ bungee jump cord tester
- ❏ nurse's aide at a home for retired Sumo wrestlers
- ❏ official physician for the National Association of Hypochondriacs
- ❏ other:_____

Bible Study / 30 Minutes

Option 1 / Gospel Study

Matthew 20:1–16 / Workers in the Vineyard

In this study we will look at a parable Jesus told about workers in a vineyard. Landowners had full-time servants who took care of the daily needs of the estate, but in busy times they would hire day laborers to help with work that the regular servants couldn't do on their own. At these times, men would gather in the village and hope that they might be hired. Read Matthew 20:1–16, and discuss the questions which follow with your group.

20 *"For the kingdom of heaven is like a landowner who went out early in the morning to hire men to work in his vineyard. ²He agreed to pay them a denarius for the day and sent them into his vineyard.*

³"About the third hour he went out and saw others standing in the marketplace doing nothing. ⁴He told them, 'You also go and work in my vine-

yard, and I will pay you whatever is right.' *So they went.

"He went out again about the sixth hour and the ninth hour and did the same thing. *About the eleventh hour he went out and found still others standing around. He asked them, 'Why have you been standing here all day long doing nothing?'

7" 'Because no one has hired us,' they answered.

"He said to them, 'You also go and work in my vineyard.'

8"When evening came, the owner of the vineyard said to his foreman, 'Call the workers and pay them their wages, beginning with the last ones hired and going on to the first.'

9"The workers who were hired about the eleventh hour came and each received a denarius. *So when those came who were hired first, they expected to receive more. But each one of them also received a denarius. *When they received it, they began to grumble against the landowner. *'These men who were hired last worked only one hour,' they said, 'and you have made them equal to us who have borne the burden of the work and the heat of the day.'

13"But he answered one of them, 'Friend, I am not being unfair to you. Didn't you agree to work for a denarius? *Take your pay and go. I want to give the man who was hired last the same as I gave you. *Don't I have the right to do what I want with my own money? Or are you envious because I am generous?'

16"So the last will be first, and the first will be last."

1. If you were one of the first workers hired (at 6 a.m.), how would you feel about what happened?
   ❑ I would never work for that jerk again!
   ❑ I would report the landowner to the Better Business Bureau!
   ❑ I would grumble behind the landowner's back.
   ❑ I wouldn't complain, because I got the pay I agreed to.
   ❑ I would be happy for the workers who got hired after I did.

2. From a business viewpoint, how would you react to the landowner's wage practices?
   ❑ He was too soft-hearted.
   ❑ He was unfair to the first workers.
   ❑ He was right—he could do whatever he wanted with his money.
   ❑ He was a compassionate employer.
   ❑ He didn't have a business mind.

3. What does this parable say to you about God and his kingdom?
   ❑ God is arbitrary and unfair.
   ❑ God's grace is truly amazing.
   ❑ God is free to bless whoever he wants.
   ❑ God's grace isn't dependent on our merit.
   ❑ God is gracious no matter how long it takes you to follow him.

4. How would you describe your attitude toward work right now?
   ❏ It's a paycheck.
   ❏ I'm not really into it—I'm not giving it my all.
   ❏ I'm giving my all—but I'm not getting much out of it.
   ❏ I'm giving my all, and find a lot of satisfaction in what I'm doing.
   ❏ I'm very fulfilled by my work.

5. What is the main reason you work?
   ❏ to survive
   ❏ to give our children a better life
   ❏ to be able to give some of my earnings
   ❏ because work is fulfilling
   ❏ because I feel called to
   ❏ other:_____

6. What do you consider the biggest challenge you face at work?
   ❏ an excessive workload?
   ❏ a difficult work environment
   ❏ balancing work with the rest of life
   ❏ feeling unfulfilled
   ❏ stretched beyond abilities
   ❏ other:_____

7. What change of attitude might help the way you feel about work?
   ❏ to stop looking at work in terms of money only
   ❏ to stop looking at those in authority as my enemy
   ❏ to look at what I can contribute rather than what I can receive
   ❏ to look for ways God can use me in my job
   ❏ to try to use my gifts in my work

8. On the following scale, how would you evaluate the sense of purpose you have at this point in your life?

1	2	3	4	5	6	7	8	9	10

   I'm just an insignificant cog in the machine of life.　　　　　　　I have a vital role in God's world.

9. Comparing your energy level and attitude about life to this parable, what "time" is it in your life right now?
   ❏ 6 a.m.—I'm raring to go.
   ❏ 9 a.m.—I'm feeling productive.
   ❏ Noon—I'm ready for a break.
   ❏ 3 p.m.—I'm running out of gas.
   ❏ 5 p.m.—Help, I *am* out of gas!
   ❏ 6 p.m.—I'm feeling satisfied with what I've accomplished.

James 4:13–17 / Future Plans

The book of James is known for its direct, even blunt, exhortations about living out the Christian faith. James is addressing Christian merchants in this part of his letter, and challenges them to do some hard reflecting on their perspectives toward their work. Read James 4:13–17 and discuss the questions with your group.

> *¹³Now listen, you who say, "Today or tomorrow we will go to this or that city, spend a year there, carry on business and make money." ¹⁴Why, you do not even know what will happen tomorrow. What is your life? You are a mist that appears for a little while and then vanishes. ¹⁵Instead, you ought to say, "If it is the Lord's will, we will live and do this or that." ¹⁶As it is, you boast and brag. All such boasting is evil. ¹⁷Anyone, then, who knows the good he ought to do and doesn't do it, sins.*

"Though a tentative outline of what God is planning for our lives is not to be avoided, an obsession with knowing everything about one's future years can deter a person from discovering God's will for today."
—Les Parrott III

1. When you were 14, what did you expect to be doing at age 24? How close were you to being right?

2. How far into the future have you planned your life?

3. How would this passage go over today as a speech to the local chamber of commerce?

4. What is wrong with the planning of the Christian merchants James is addressing here (see first and third notes on v. 13)?

5. How easy is it for you to have the outlook James calls for in verse 15?

6. Is James putting down long-range planning altogether (see notes on v. 15)? Is he against making a profit?

7. What might James have in mind in verse 17 when he mentions these businessmen's "sins of omission" (see second note on v. 17)?

8. Take a moment to reflect on how verse 17 is true for your life, particularly when it comes to your work and career planning. What situation or issue comes to mind, and what is usually the reason you don't do what you know you should?

9. What does this passage say to you about the plans you are making for your future? Where do you need God's guidance?

Caring Time / 15–45 Minutes

Take time at the close to share any personal prayer requests. Answer the question:

"How can we help you in prayer this week?"

Then go around and let each person pray for the person on their right. Finish the sentence:

"Dear God, I want to speak to you about my friend _____."

Reference Notes

Summary. James begins discussion of his third and final theme: testing. He will deal with this theme, at first, as it touches the issue of wealth. The problem is the difficulty that comes with being wealthy and the tensions this brings, both on a personal level and for the whole community. In this first part of his discussion (4:13–17), he looks at the situation of a group of Christian businessmen—in particular, at their "sins of omission."

4:13 Boasting about what will happen tomorrow is an example of human arrogance. It is arrogant because God is the only one who knows what will happen in the future.

Now listen. This is literally "Come now." It stands in sharp contrast to the way James has been addressing his readers. In the previous section he called them "my brothers" (3:1,11). James reverts to this more impersonal language in addressing these merchants.

"Today or tomorrow we will go ..." James lets us listen in on the plans of a group of businessmen. Possibly they are looking at a map together. In any case, they are planning for the future and are concerned with where they will go, how long they will stay, what they will do, and how much profit they will make. It appears to be an innocent conversation. "In trade a person has to plan ahead: Travel plans, market projections, time frames, profit forecasts are the stuff of business in all ages. Every honest merchant would plan in exactly the same way—pagan, Jew or Christian—and that is exactly the problem James has with these plans: There is absolutely nothing about their desires for the future, their use of money or their way of doing business that is any different from the rest of the world. Their worship may be exemplary, their personal morality, impeccable; but when it comes to business they think entirely on a worldly plane" (Davids, GNC).

we will go. Travel by traders in the first century usually took the form of caravan or ship. There were no hard and fast time tables. Instead, one had to wait until the right transportation came along going in your direction. However, there were certain seasons when ships sailed and caravans were more likely to travel.

carry on business. The word James uses here is derived from the Greek word *emporos*, from which the English word "emporium" comes. It denotes wholesale merchants who traveled from city to city, buying and selling. A different word was used to describe local peddlers who had small businesses in the bazaars. The growth of cities and the increase of trade between them during the Greco-Roman era created great opportunities for making money. In the Bible a certain distrust of traders is sometimes expressed (see Prov. 20:23; Amos 8:4–6; Rev. 18:11–20).

4:14 *tomorrow.* All such planning presupposes that tomorrow will unfold like any other day, when in fact, the future is anything but secure (see Prov. 27:1).

What is your life? Is it not death that is the great unknown? Who can know when death will come and interrupt plans? "Their projections are made; their plans are laid. But it all hinges on a will higher than theirs, a God unconsulted in their planning. That very night disease might strike; suddenly their plans evaporate, their only trip being one on a bier to a cold grave. They are like the rich fool of Jesus' parable, who had made a large honest profit through the chance occurrences of farming. Feeling secure, he makes rational plans for a comfortable retirement. 'But God said to him, "You fool! This very night you will have to give up your life" ' (Luke 12:16–21). By thinking on the worldly plane, James' Christian business people have gained a false sense of security. They need to look death in the face and realize their lack of control over life" (Davids, GNC).

mist. Hosea 13:3 says: "Therefore they will be like the morning mist, like the early dew that disappears, like chaff swirling from a threshing floor, like smoke escaping through a window."

4:15 *"If it is the Lord's will."* This phrase (often abbreviated D.V. after its Latin form) is not used in the Old Testament, though it was found frequently in Greek and Roman literature and is used by Paul (see Acts 18:21; 1 Cor. 4:19; 16:7). The uncertainty of the future ought not to be a terror to the Christian. Instead, it ought to force on him or her an awareness of how dependent a person is upon God, and thus move that person to a planning that involves God.

we will live and do this or that. James is not ruling out planning. He says plan, but keep God in mind.

4:16 In contrast to such prayerful planning, these Christian merchants are very proud of what they do on their own. James is not condemning international trade as such, nor the wealth it produced. (His comments on riches come in 5:1–3.) What he is concerned about is that all this is done without reference to God, in a spirit of boastful arrogance.

boast. The problem with this boasting is that they are claiming to have the future under control when, in fact, it is God who holds time in his hands. These are empty claims.

brag. This word originally described an itinerant quack who touted "cures" that did not work. It came to mean claiming to be able to do something that you could not do.

4:17 Some feel that this proverb-like statement may, in fact, be a saying of Jesus that did not get recorded in the Gospel accounts. In any case, by it James points out the nature of so-called "sins of omission." In other words, it is sin when we fail to do what we ought to do. The more familiar definition is of "sins of commission" or wrongdoing (see 1 John 3:4). In other words, sinning can be both active and passive. Christians can sin by doing what they ought not to do (law-breaking); or by not doing what they know they should do (failure).

who knows the good. James applies this principle to the merchants. It is not that they are cheating and stealing in the course of their business (that would be active wrongdoing). The problem is in what they fail to do. Generally James defines "the good" as acts of charity toward those in need. And certainly in the context of this letter, it would appear that these men are failing in their duty to the poor. "James, then, may be suggesting that they plan like the world because they are motivated by the world, for God has his own way to invest money: give it to the poor (Matt. 6:19–21). If they took God into account they might not be trying to increase their own standard of living; God might lead them to relieve the suffering around them, that is, to do good" (Davids, GNC).

P.S.
If the next session is going to be your last session together, you may want to plan a party to celebrate your time together. Save a few minutes at the close of this session to make these plans.

SESSION

7

Having a Servant Mind

3-PART AGENDA

ICE-BREAKER
15 Minutes

BIBLE STUDY
30 Minutes

CARING TIME
15–45 Minutes

When work is a means to self-aggrandizement, then each person is in it for themselves. The issues become: "What is easiest for me?"; "What will advance my well-being?"; and "How can I get more money out of this?" The results of such self-focus are problematical in several ways. First of all, it is bad for our society. Product reliability suffers because it is always easier for a worker to take a shortcut than to do the job right. Consumer needs are considered only when there is a commercial advantage to do so. Worker loyalty becomes a thing of the past. It is also bad, however, for us as individuals. We can no longer take pride in our work, and we no longer see what we do as meaningful.

> **LEADER: Read the bottom part of page M8 in the center section concerning future mission possibilities for your group. Save plenty of time for the evaluation and future planning during the Caring Time. You will need to be prepared to lead this important discussion.**

It has been commonly thought that what each person should seek is individual self-fulfillment. But many people have found that search to be a dead-end street. Self-fulfillment can only come when we see our work as a meaningful contribution to something beyond ourself.

What we need then, is a revival of the servant mind—an attitude where we work to serve our world and the people around us. In this session, we will consider what it means to have a servant mind. In Option 1 (from the Gospel of John), we will consider the example Jesus gave his disciples when he washed their feet. In our Option 2 Study (from Paul's letter to the Philippians), we will consider how Jesus set an example for us by taking on both the form and the attitude of a servant.

55

Ice-Breaker / 15 Minutes

The Right Tools. One of the most important tasks for people who work with their hands is to recognize what the right tool is for the job. Over these past sessions, we have done an important job—the job of building community while we explore our vocation. Every person in this group has been a "tool" who has been used in that building process. In silence, think about the members of this group. Jot down their names next to the "tools" that described them during these sessions. (It's okay if you choose the same tool for more than one person.) Then ask one person to listen while the others explain where they put that person's name. Then go to the next person and do the same until everyone has been affirmed.

_____HAMMER: The one who drove home a point that stuck with you.

_____SAW: The one who always cut to the heart of the matter.

_____PLANE: The one who was there to "smooth things over" when there was tension.

_____GLASSES: The one who helped us see things clearly.

_____BRACE: The one who gave us support.

_____HINGE: The one who gave our group flexibility.

_____LEVEL: The one who brought in a good balance.

_____HOT GLUE: The one who helped us stick together.

_____SANDPAPER: The one God used to work on our "rough edges."

Bible Study / 30 Minutes

Option 1 / Gospel Study

John 13:1–17 / The Example of Christ

The following passage describes an event during the Last Supper which Jesus celebrated with his disciples on the night before his death. It was customary for people's dusty, sandaled feet to be washed, usually by the lowest-ranking servant, before a meal was served. Read John 13:1–17 and discuss the questions which follow with your group.

13 *It was just before the Passover Feast. Jesus knew that the time had come for him to leave this world and go to the Father. Having loved his own who were in the world, he now showed them the full extent of his love.*

²The evening meal was being served, and the devil had already prompted Judas Iscariot, son of Simon, to betray Jesus. ³Jesus knew that the Father had put all things under his power, and that he had come from God and was returning to God; ⁴so he got up from the meal, took off his outer clothing, and wrapped a towel around his waist. ⁵After that, he poured water into a basin and began to wash his disciples' feet, drying them with the towel that was wrapped around him.

⁶He came to Simon Peter, who said to him, "Lord, are you going to wash my feet?"

⁷Jesus replied, "You do not realize now what I am doing, but later you will understand."

⁸"No," said Peter, "you shall never wash my feet."

Jesus answered, "Unless I wash you, you have no part with me."

⁹"Then, Lord," Simon Peter replied, "not just my feet but my hands and my head as well!"

¹⁰Jesus answered, "A person who has had a bath needs only to wash his feet; his whole body is clean. And you are clean, though not every one of you." ¹¹For he knew who was going to betray him, and that was why he said not every one was clean.

¹²When he had finished washing their feet, he put on his clothes and returned to his place. "Do you understand what I have done for you?" he asked them. ¹³"You call me 'Teacher' and 'Lord,' and rightly so, for that is what I am. ¹⁴Now that I, your Lord and Teacher, have washed your feet, you also should wash one another's feet. ¹⁵I have set you an example that you should do as I have done for you. ¹⁶I tell you the truth, no servant is greater than his master, nor is a messenger greater than the one who sent him. ¹⁷Now that you know these things, you will be blessed if you do them."

1. Why didn't the disciples wash their feet before supper?
   ❐ They forgot.
   ❐ They felt clean enough.
   ❐ It wasn't their job.
   ❐ There weren't any servants around.

2. Why did Jesus wash his disciples' feet?
   ❐ to humble them
   ❐ to be an example of servanthood
   ❐ to illustrate his whole mission
   ❐ to show them real leadership
   ❐ to show his deep love for them before he died
   ❐ to give them a new model for their life together

3. What would you have done if you had been there and Jesus approached you to wash your feet?
   - ❒ left the room
   - ❒ refused to let him
   - ❒ broken down and cried
   - ❒ felt honored by his caring act
   - ❒ just sat there—feeling guilty and unworthy
   - ❒ jumped up and tried to wash *his* feet

4. When you were in the seventh grade, what kind of servant-tasks were you required to do around the house?
   - ❒ make my bed
   - ❒ help with cooking
   - ❒ clean my room
   - ❒ do laundry
   - ❒ take out the trash
   - ❒ dust and vacuum
   - ❒ wash the dishes
   - ❒ all of the above
   - ❒ look after my sibling(s)
   - ❒ none of the above
   - ❒ do yard work
   - ❒ other:_____

5. What do you do for your family right now which is most like "washing feet"—a somewhat unpleasant, humble servant-task? How do you feel about doing this?

6. What do you do at your job that is most like "washing feet"? How does Jesus' example affect your attitude about this task?

7. Which of the following is true in relationship to your present job and servanthood?
   - ❒ My job has nothing to do with serving—it's about making money.
   - ❒ My job requires many servant-tasks, most of them are pleasant.
   - ❒ My job requires many servant-tasks, most of which are unpleasant.
   - ❒ The main pleasure I get from my job comes from serving people.
   - ❒ I chose my job specifically so I wouldn't have to do unpleasant tasks like that.
   - ❒ Jesus' example of servanthood is what keeps me going in my job.

8. In general, what's holding you back from living a life of service like Jesus demonstrated and taught?
   - ❒ I'm afraid I'll be taken advantage of.
   - ❒ I don't have time.
   - ❒ I'm not willing to do things that aren't "my job."
   - ❒ I haven't had many good role models.
   - ❒ I guess I'm too selfish.
   - ❒ other:_____

9. What is one way you can serve someone else this coming week?

Philippians 2:1–11 / The Attitude of Christ

Throughout his letters, the apostle Paul takes care to not be seen as boastful or self-serving, but to be seen as a servant of Christ. In the following passage, he advises his readers to do the same thing by imitating Christ. One of the reasons Paul wrote his letter to the Philippians was to exhort them regarding unity. In the first part of this passage, he instructs the believers at Philippi that unity is achieved by self-sacrificing humility. Then, in the last part of the passage (which was most likely an early Christian hymn), Paul lifts up Jesus as the supreme example of such humility. Read Philippians 2:1–11 and discuss the questions which follow with your group.

2 *If you have any encouragement from being united with Christ, if any comfort from his love, if any fellowship with the Spirit, if any tenderness and compassion, ²then make my joy complete by being like-minded, having the same love, being one in spirit and purpose. ³Do nothing out of selfish ambition or vain conceit, but in humility consider others better than yourselves. ⁴Each of you should look not only to your own interests, but also to the interests of others.*
⁵Your attitude should be the same as that of Christ Jesus:

⁶Who, being in very nature God,
*   did not consider equality with God something to be grasped,*
⁷but made himself nothing,
*   taking the very nature of a servant,*
*   being made in human likeness.*
⁸And being found in appearance as a man,
*   he humbled himself*
*   and became obedient to death—*
*   even death on a cross!*
⁹Therefore God exalted him to the highest place
*   and gave him the name that is above every name,*
¹⁰that at the name of Jesus every knee should bow,
*   in heaven and on earth and under the earth,*
¹¹and every tongue confess that Jesus Christ is Lord,
*   to the glory of God the Father.*

1. If you had your very own personal servant, what would be the first job for them on your list?

2. What does it mean to consider someone "better than yourself" (v. 3)? How does humility differ from being a doormat?

USE THE FOLLOWING SCALE FOR QUESTIONS 3–6:

1	2	3	4	5	6	7	8	9	10
my own interests always first								the interests of others always first	

3. From this passage (and your own understanding), where do you think the best balance is between "looking to your own interests" and "looking to the interests of others" (v. 4)? _____

4. What attitude prevailed in the home where you were raised? _____

5. Where do you think the attitude of most people you know lies? _____

6. Judging by your present lifestyle, what score would you give yourself? _____

7. How do you feel after reading verses 6–11? Although the emphasis in these verses is on Jesus' humility, what else stands out about him in this passage?

8. If you embraced the attitude of Christ, how would that affect your present job?
   ❒ I would have to leave it.
   ❒ It would eventually get me fired.
   ❒ It might cut our profit, but it would improve our service.
   ❒ It would make my work more meaningful.
   ❒ It would make me more sensitive to the people I work with.
   ❒ other:_____

9. Where in your life do you struggle with reflecting the attitude of Christ? At home? At work? Other? What is one thing you can commit to this week that will help you meet this challenge?

Caring Time / 15–45 Minutes

1. Take some time to evaluate the life of your group by using the statements below. Read the first sentence out loud and ask everyone to explain where they would put a dot between the two extremes. When you are finished, go back and give your group an overall grade in the categories of Group Building, Bible Study and Mission.

GROUP BUILDING

On celebrating life and having fun together, we were more like a ...
wet blanket _____**hot tub**

On becoming a caring community, we were more like a ...
prickly porcupine _____**cuddly teddy bear**

BIBLE STUDY

On sharing our spiritual stories, we were more like a ...
shallow pond _____**spring-fed lake**

On digging into Scripture, we were more like a ...
slow-moving snail _____**voracious anteater**

○→○ MISSION

On inviting new people into our group, we were more like a ...
barbed-wire fence _____**wide-open door**

On stretching our vision for mission, we were more like an ...
ostrich _____**eagle**

2. What are some specific areas in which you have grown in this course about your gifts and calling?
❐ deepening my appreciation for God's call in my life
❐ learning how to discern God's call and God's will
❐ discovering new insights about my spiritual gifts
❐ acquiring a strategy for developing my gifts further
❐ gaining confidence to take risks in investing my life
❐ understanding the connection between my work and God's will
❐ sparking a desire in my life to be a servant
❐ other:_____

A covenant is a promise made to each other in the presence of God. Its purpose is to indicate your intention to make yourselves available to one another for the fulfillment of the purposes you share in common. If your group is going to continue, in a spirit of prayer work your way through the following sentences, trying to reach an agreement on each statement pertaining to your ongoing life together. Write out your covenant like a contract, stating your purpose, goals and the ground rules for your group.

1. The purpose of our group will be:

2. Our goals will be:

3. We will meet for _____weeks, after which we will decide if we wish to continue as a group.

4. We will meet from _____ to _____ and we will strive to start on time and end on time.

5. We will meet at _____ (place) or we will rotate from house to house.

6. We will agree to the following ground rules for our group (check):

❐ PRIORITY: While you are in the course, you give the group meetings priority.

❐ PARTICIPATION: Everyone participates and no one dominates.

❐ RESPECT: Everyone is given the right to their own opinion, and all questions are encouraged and respected.

❐ CONFIDENTIALITY: Anything that is said in the meeting is never repeated outside the meeting.

❐ EMPTY CHAIR: The group stays open to new people at every meeting, as long as they understand the ground rules.

❐ SUPPORT: Permission is given to call upon each other in time of need at any time.

❐ ACCOUNTABILITY: We agree to let the members of the group hold us accountable to the commitments which each of us make in whatever loving ways we decide upon.

❐ MISSION: We will do everything in our power to start a new group.

Summary. Paul is writing to the Philippians to urge them to act in humility and without selfish ambition. He points to Christ as an example. Through Paul's eyes we see Jesus, the divine Savior who comes to his people in humility not in power; we see the Lord of the Universe before whom all bow choosing to die for his subjects; we see one who is in nature God, voluntarily descending to the depths (and becoming a servant) before he is lifted up to the heights (and assumes his kingship).

2:1 *If.* In Greek, this construction assumes a positive response, e.g., "If you have any encouragement, as of course you do ... ." By means of four clauses, Paul urges the Philippians to say "Yes" to his request that they live together in harmony.

2:2 *like-minded.* This is literally: "think the same way." However, Paul is not just urging everyone to hold identical ideas and opinions. Paul is calling for a far deeper form of unity than simple doctrinal conformity.

2:3 *selfish ambition.* This means working to advance oneself without thought for others. The road to unity is via the path of humble self-sacrifice.

humility. Christians are to accord others the same dignity and respect that Christ has given to all people. Humility involves seeing others not on the basis of how clever, attractive, or pious they are, but through the eyes of Christ (who died for them).

2:4 *look not only to your own interests.* Preoccupation with personal interests, along with selfish ambition and vain conceit, make unity impossible. Individualism or partisanship work against community. Note that Paul says "look *not only* to your own interests." Personal interests are important (although not to the exclusion of everything else).

2:5 This is the transition verse between the exhortation of 2:1–4 and the illustration of 2:6–11. In it Paul states that the model for the sort of self-sacrificing humility he has been urging is found in Jesus.

2:6–11 To demonstrate the humility of Christ, Paul quotes from an ancient Christian hymn about Jesus. Perhaps he composed the hymn himself. In quoting this hymn, Paul provides a fascinating glimpse into how the early Christians viewed Jesus. He also gives us one of the few existing examples of early church hymnology. There is little agreement between scholars as to how this hymn breaks into verses or how it is to be phrased. However, one thing is clear. The hymn has two equal parts. Part one (vv. 6–8) focuses on the self-humiliation of Jesus. Part two (vv. 9–11) focuses on God's exaltation of Jesus. In part one, Jesus is the subject of the two main verbs, while in part two God is the subject of the two main verbs.

2:6 *being.* This is not the normal Greek word for "being." "It describes that which a man is in his very essence, that which cannot be changed" (Barclay). This word also carries the idea of pre-existence. By using it, Paul is saying that Jesus always existed in the form of God.

very nature. The Greek word here is *morphe* (used twice by Paul in this hymn). He says that Jesus was "in very nature God," and that he then took upon himself "the very nature of a servant." This is a key word in understanding the nature of Christ.

to be grasped. This is a rare word, used only at this point in the New Testament. It refers to the fact that Jesus did not have to "snatch" equality with God. It was his already, and thus he could give it away. Giving, not grasping, is what Jesus did.

2:7 *made himself nothing.* Literally, "to empty," or "to pour out until the container is empty."

being made. In contrast to the verb in verse 6 (which stresses Christ's eternal nature), this verb points to the fact that at a particular time he was born in the likeness of a human being.

human likeness. The point is not that Jesus just seemed to be human. He assumed the identity of a person and was similar in all ways to other human beings.

2:8 *he humbled himself.* This is the central point that Paul wants to make. This is why he offered this illustration. Jesus is the ultimate model of one who lived a life of self-sacrifice, self-renunciation, and self-surrender. Jesus existed at the pinnacle and yet descended to the very base. There has never been a more radical humbling. Furthermore, this was not something forced upon Jesus. This was voluntarily chosen by Christ.

death on a cross. For a Jew there was no more humiliating way to die. Jesus, who was equal to God, died like an accused criminal. His descent from glory had brought him as low as one could go.

2:10 *Jesus.* The one before whom Christians will stand at the Last Judgment is not an anonymous Life Force, but the man of Galilee who has a familiar face.

bow. Everyone will one day pay homage to Jesus. This worship will come from all of creation—all angels (in heaven), all people (on earth), and all demons (under the earth).

2:11 *Jesus Christ is Lord.* The climax of this hymn. This is the earliest and most basic confession of faith on the part of the church (see Acts 2:36; Rom. 10:9; 1 Cor. 12:3).